T0103773

DOHA!

DOHA!

Diary of a Delhi-O-holic

ANAM ARSALAN

PARTRIDGE

To order additional copies of this book, contact
Partridge India
000 800 10062 62
orders.india@partridgepublishing.com

www.partridgepublishing.com/india

CONTENTS

To
Hina, Nashrah, little Nameer,
Ammi & Abbu

ACKNOWLEDGMENTS

For the number of people involved in turning my dream into a reality, I suppose this should be the most difficult exercise. First and foremost, I must thank my Publishers – Partridge India, in helping me putting those words into print. Secondly, I owe it all to my office, the Qatar Sports Press Committee for letting me dream on.

Much like the character of *Doha! Diary of a Delhi-O-holic*, the people associated with it are spread across the four corners of the world.

Also, since the Publishers had their offices spanning the globe, I got to interact with their representatives everywhere. Be it Kolkata, Indianapolis or Cebu City, their network is truly ubiquitous. Gemma Ramos, Emily Laurel, Yanessa Evans, Mark Angelo, Marvin Canada, and Ged Allan Negradas, it really was a pleasure working with you.

Richa Saxena, your proofreading was spot on. A copy editor with a legal background, such as yours, is a definite plus. Not to forget, you were the one who introduced me to the illustrators, Jayanti (Shuchi) Asthana and Swathy Mohan, who did a fabulous job.

While Richa is based in the suburbs of New Delhi, Shuchi, an avid cartoonist, is an engineering graduate from Kanpur. Swathy, a celebrity sketch artist lives and works as a software engineer in Chennai.

Shahjahan Moidin and Mustafa Abu Munes, I am truly indebted to you for providing me those timely and impressive pictures. Shahjahan, originally from Thrissur, but working in Doha took the breath-taking shot of Al Corniche, which has been showcased on the cover of the book. Jordanian Mustafa's action shot of Chinese Paralympian Zhou Hongzhuan formed the basis of Swathy's sketch in Chapter, 'That incredible man who held my hand'.

Also, I think the idiom, 'don't judge a book by its cover,' is only for the keeps, as everyone knows how attracted we are to books that have dazzling covers. That's where you score, Naveen Siromoni. Your cover design was beyond compare.

Words 'thank you' sound shallow in front of Keir Radnedge. The highly acclaimed journalist and the Association Internationale de la Presse Sportive (AIPS) Football Commission Chairman, who took time out to pen down the Foreword, has authored the comprehensive 'The 2010 FIFA World Cup South Africa Official Book', among others.

My journalist and author friend for more than a decade, Suvam Pal, your honest opinion came in handy while penning down the 'About the Author'. Otherwise, it could have been a challenging task, for I don't always enjoy writing about myself.

While Keir is from London, Suvam, an NRI himself, is currently based in Beijing and is associated with CCTV.

Finally, a big thank you to those who said, "You write well!" or "You should write a book".

FOREWORD

Qatar is different. It's not Dubai, selling itself into the tourist market. Qatar is business. Business of its own. Business of the world.

Hence the focus on major sports events which I have witnessed in visiting over the past two decades.

Every week a new championship of one sort or another, one sport or another.

The visitor sees the event, the bright new venues, the stadium opulence born of today's money rather than yesteryear's history.

Football, swimming, tennis, handball, golf, cycling. These and many more. They offer an impressive veneer, painted on the outer skin of the complex, hidden society within.

That is where *Anam Arsalan* steps in. And between.

For foreign journalists he has been a 'local' man bridging that sports media gap. The international touch but with the domestic official perspective.

Hence the fascination of this memoir, surely only an interim version.

How did an outsider come to work in Qatar? What are the irritations and the pleasures?

Who comprise the cast of fellow expatriates, all with myriad challenges of their own? The Aditis, the Adels and the rest.

Here is an entertaining glimpse into another world; a Qatar the visiting world can never see beyond the clichéd headlines.

A glimpse down into another Gulf.

Keir Radnedge
(Author of 33 books and highly-acclaimed The 2010 FIFA World Cup South Africa Official Book)
20.05.16

PREFACE

"*Yaar!* Do you know a person who has good sports knowledge and is willing to go to Qatar," said a voice over the phone.

"You won't have to look too far," I replied.

That's where it all began.

My bags lay packed for over a month before the visa, tickets, and the employment offer arrived. Well! I was told to be ready for a speedy journey and hence the early packing.

I received a government visa, and I was to enter Doha as a 'Government Official' – pretty impressive indeed, but what caught my attention was the employment offer, which was printed in Arabic.

It was then that a series of referrals with my dear learned friends and translators began. Until, at last, the document was sent to my in-laws in Lucknow, where it was translated into Urdu. Alas! The person who 'decoded' the copy was so well-read that his Urdu looked more like Arabic.

Soon the translated version passed through the hands of my wife, my father and also the *Imam* of the nearby mosque. By all means, I did manage to gather those bits and pieces of information, before the agency from where I had received the call and which was responsible for sending me to Doha, got ready with their English version; unluckily, that too wasn't conclusive.

Finally, it was decided that I grab the opportunity. With a prayer on my lips and stars in my eyes, I went forth and boarded the Qatar Airways flight No. QR 565 to Doha. On the morning of 11th October, after a 2-hour 40-minute flight, I landed at the state-of-the-art Hamad International Airport.

A gentleman wearing a *thob* (Arabic dress) with a cap was there at the Airport to receive me. He dropped me at the hotel Doha Downtown, which was to be my destination for more than a month.

Sleepy and jetlagged, I approached the girl at the reception, but a rude shock shook me out of slumber. The girl from the Philippines told me that there wasn't a booking in my name. Shocked out of my wits, I could just utter, "What?"

I pulled out the phone from the front pocket and then followed a series of anxious phone calls. The duty manager, an Egyptian, was rather compassionate. "Sir,

I understand your plight," he said. "I always try to put myself in the other person's shoes." He suggested that I occupy a room, and things would soon be settled. Too anxious to do that I stayed at the reception even as phone calls and chats over WhatsApp Messenger continued for more than two hours.

Incidentally, I had faced exactly the same situation in 2007, when as a correspondent for the *Hindustan Times* I had travelled to Shanghai to cover the Special Olympics. The agency sponsoring the trip hadn't made any hotel booking in my name, and I had to call up New Delhi to iron out the glitches.

The issue at Doha Downtown was resolved when I spoke to the general manager of the hotel, a Pakistani gentleman who told me that the booking had been done. Unfortunately, the person who had made the booking hadn't spelt my name correctly and that caused the confusion.

No sooner was the issue resolved that I was led to a cosy studio apartment. With my baggage safe, I stepped out and headed to the nearest currency exchange counter.

The local time was 5:30 pm, but it seemed like night; maybe a reflection of the tough day I had endured. Only an evening earlier, I had taken my 6-year-old daughter for a bike ride and now I was miles away from home. Her sweet little nothings were still ringing in my ear as I proceeded to buy a local SIM card.

The day had been hard, but the night was easy and soothing. Post the fine dining experience in my hotel room, I was sound asleep.

The next day I was to get a call that would eventually chart the course of my life in Doha.

Anam Arsalan
(Doha)

BELLISSIMO MUBARAK

"Where have I landed?"

I woke up to completely unfamiliar surroundings. The amnesia had lasted a millisecond, before images from yesterday made me feel lonely and gloomy. Homesick and tired, I dragged myself from the comfortable bed and decided to prepare for another demanding day. Stepping out of room number 121, I headed towards Town Café, the hotel's restaurant.

I had just drawn a bite from a large apple when the waitress, a smartly dressed Filipino, told me that the 'free breakfast' wasn't for me. Apparently, I was a 'budget guest' for the supposedly 'starred' hotel and the breakfast, that is usually complementary in most hotels, didn't exactly go with my profile.

"So, what do I do?" I asked, feeling somewhat embarrassed. "Sir, you can order the breakfast in your room."

I decided not to brood over the issue and went straight to my room on the first floor and ordered the continental meal. The mouth-watering delicacies were a sheer gastronomical delight.

No sooner had I satisfied my taste buds that the pangs of nostalgia came back to strike me down with renewed vigour. Alone and confused, I randomly looked up the contacts on my phone. That's when I noticed the name of a senior official from the Qatar Sports Press Committee.

Post the customary "Hello" and "I hope the hotel is to your liking", words of reassurances, "don't worry, everything will be sorted out soon…" provided the much-needed comfort that had eluded me for long.

The phone went silent, and then there was a long lull. It must have been a couple of hours before I got another reassuring phone call.

"*Ello!* Mr. Arsalan, my name is Mubarak. I am calling from the Qatar Sports Press Committee. I would come to your hotel to meet you, today. Whatever it takes or how long it gets, I would definitely be there," said the voice from the other end.

At 7 pm, that night, Mubarak, a Qatari Arab, was waiting in his SUV in front of the hotel. There was an unmarked air of sophistication about the man with gentle manners, who would have been in his mid-forties.

Around the same time I was to meet a gentleman from the agency that was involved in bringing me to Doha.

Mubarak was waiting in his SUV. There was an unmarked air of sophistication about him.

The Good Samaritan was not just generous enough to take me to the Hilton where the representative of the agency was supposed to meet me, but he also led me on a guided tour of Al Corniche, the uptown Doha locality lined with skyscrapers that gleamed in the night, presenting a spectacular picture.

Al Corniche, the waterfront promenade that extends miles along the Doha Bay also houses the Qatar Olympic Committee office, where a 'dotted line' on a particular paper awaited my signature.

Another round of delicacies was rather befitting with the situation and the occasion. I guess, I had ordered for a carrot cake. Now, the cake wasn't made out of carrot, but had a miniature carrot carving above it, and that's why the name. I am not certain, who footed the bill, but it surely wasn't me.

As we chatted over some light refreshments, a realisation dawned upon me that this tiny, wealthy Arabian Gulf nation was fast emerging as a sporting destination in the region. In time, I was to witness Doha stage and win bids for premier sporting events from across the platter. No wonder, a whole new city is being built around the 'Sport for Life' concept, which happens to be the motto of the Qatar Olympic Committee.

Doha unlike Dubai won't enchant you with shopping festivals, expos or marts, but it definitely has the magic wand that turns sporting events into festivals for 'sportaholics'. Talking about festivals, the agent pointed out how he had enjoyed the Eid al-Adha festivities and would be returning home to New Delhi to be with his family during Diwali. That's when I came to know that Mubarak had recently returned from Hajj, a pilgrimage that is mandatory for every financially stable and capable Muslim.

All this while I could not stop noticing how impeccably he was dressed. It was rather late, but his pure white *thob* was as clean as it would have been when it had arrived from the laundry.

Though he wore the traditional Arabic dress, those Versace cufflinks, and Bvlgari watch were a give-away. Clearly, Mubarak was more than just a 'financially stable Muslim'.

Later, that night he dropped me at my hotel in Al Sadd and even had a word with the duty manager. The duo spoke in Arabic, but it was clear that the discussion revolved around my stay. After all, I was supposed to be in Doha for good.

As he turned around and said goodbye, I asked him for his visiting card. I couldn't figure out a better way of knowing his other initials.

But the "Sorry, I am not carrying one!" caught me on the wrong foot...

Next morning, a spanking sedan driven by a young man was meandering its way through rush hour traffic; it's destination – the Indian High Commission. Yousuf, like most affluent but traditional Qataris, looked elegant in a *thob,* even as an avant-garde brand of shades covered his eyes.

His dexterous driving was dotted with sudden finger movements flipping the sides of his *keffiyeh* that would 'mischievously' make their way onto his face. "Amazing how a traditional wear of the Arabian Gulf, with slight adjustments, had transformed into a fashion statement that would stretch beyond aeons and borders..."

"Do you know the way ahead?" asked Yousuf. "Looks like, the GPS is somewhat misleading."

Mubarak, the workaholic, had directed his nephew, Yousuf, to accompany me (read lead me) to the Indian Embassy where my certificates required attestation.

"Let me figure it out," I said, as my fingers went for Ahmed Junaid's number on the keypad.

I had met Ahmed at the Terminal 3 of the IGI Airport in New Delhi. Rather relaxed, he had made himself comfortable on a lounge near the departure gate. I went and occupied the one adjoining him, and soon we busy chitchatting.

There was a common chord, though. He came from the same city where my wife, Hina, had resided before she took the plunge and shifted base on the outskirts of New Delhi, with me in the two, most certainly.

"Look around for the petrol pump and the *Gulf Times* office," said Ahmed. "Those are the landmarks."

No sooner had the phone gone silent that the young Qatari beside me made his way to the petrol pump. A few more enquiries and we could see the newspaper office.

"Ah! In Arabic, it's called the *Al Raya*," exclaimed Yousuf. "Had you said that, I would have taken you straight to your destination."

The smile that had made its way across my face almost immediately faded. It was 11 am and a long queue greeted me at the counter.

Worried, if I would ever be able to see the pretty lady at the counter, who gave away tokens, I dialled 'M'.

Mubarak, though busy, made a few phone calls to the higher ups and I managed to sneak in past the guard, who failed to gauge the anxiety that was effectively masked by my confident look. Also, the words "Qatar Sports Press Committee" did wonders, but the man at the reception was unmoved.

Eventually, I did manage to collect the coveted token. Luckily, the crowd had dwindled making the procedure easier for me.

Finally, my certificates were checked by an officer at another counter, and the duplicate copies admitted for attestation, which I was to collect later in the day. I hadn't realised then that I was committing a huge folly getting all those certificates attested and that too the duplicate ones. I ended up paying through the nose for those 15 documents, which ultimately would be rendered worthless.

On our way back to the hotel, I came to know that Yousuf, held a Master's degree in management. And, like his uncle Mubarak, he too had studied in London.

At 4 pm, when the time for the collection of certificates approached, my phone bell rang. "Should I come over to pick you up?" Yousuf asked politely.

"No, it's okay. I can make it on my own." I said, and decided to take a taxi to save him the trouble.

The collection wasn't an issue, but what came next would eventually leave me utterly exhausted and sapped.

I was advised by fellow 'bystanders' not to take the taxi standing in front of the Embassy gates as they charge exorbitant rates and refuse to follow the meter.

Taking note, I walked towards the main road, but could not spot a single taxi, which was willing to take me to Al Sadd as per the meter readings.

I walked for an hour even as the sky changed colours. From *'Into the Blue'* to the *'Fifty Shades of Grey'*, to *'Pitch Black'*, I had witnessed them all. To my bad luck, the taxi never came my way.

It would have been close to two hours before a Nepalese driver stopped. He was already carrying a passenger aboard, but it looked like my sullen and weary face made him take pity. Or was he keen on making some fast buck, I wouldn't know.

As I alighted my cash-strapped wallet suddenly went feather light. But, I could hear my sore limbs say, "thank you."

The following day, misery struck me like a hailstorm. Last night's arduous trek had taken its toll. I felt tired, ill and exhausted and couldn't make myself ready for another rough ride, which involved my presence at the expatriate affairs office, some 20 kilometres from Doha Downtown.

Even as I was contemplating my next move, Yousuf arrived, this time in a gas-guzzling SUV. The decent young man not only sympathised at my condition, he agreed to take those certificates to the passport office.

I woke up, startled; the phone was buzzing. It was Yousuf at the other end. He was back and waiting for me at the hotel entrance.

Lumbering, I made my way towards the entrance for the news that would leave me zapped. "My friend!" he laboured on, "You will have to get your original certificates attested from your foreign ministry office in India."

Flabbergasted, I just stood there.

The news was yet to sink in, but he had gone, long gone. Though, ifs and buts remained!

--x--

Thank God for Google!

"You need to get my certificates attested from India. That is a must for starting work here," I said, trying to hide the agitation and anxiety in my voice.

"Hmm, so are we supposed to get that done? Is it not their (my office) job?"

The woman on the other end was trying to steer clear of the administrative lacuna left wide open by her agency. It took me a while to make her understand that the visit visa was worthless. I wasn't vacationing in Doha, after all.

Fortunately, the agency's chief, who was based in Doha then, was more forthcoming. He not only took my papers back for attestation during his Diwali visit but also promised speedy resolution of the issue.

In the meantime, I signed the dotted line and started work, even though I knew that it would take a while before the salary would be credited to my account, which too I didn't have.

Luckily, the top bosses, even those who were rarely visible, were always ready to dip their fingers into their wallets to keep my financial troubles at bay. Not to forget, the 400 dollars that the agency had lent came in handy. A large chunk of that money, however, went towards family sustenance and monthly mortgage payoff, also known as the EMI (Equated Monthly Installment).

So there I was, starting life afresh but, the financial baggage from the past continued to slow me down.

After Mubarak had read out the details of my employment offer, in English of course, he led me to my work station.

The office was a fairly large one and offered an impressive view of the Doha Bay or the Al Corniche. The chairman's room flaunted exquisitely crafted interiors with enough room for leisure seating and enclosures for meetings. I occupied a chair in the corresponding room well-equipped with amenities and office equipment.

Though there were four work stations, there was just one other person besides Mubarak and me, who were present there.

The Egyptian, Mustafa, well into his 50s, had been an old workhorse of the Qatar Sports Press Committee. Although a colleague, I took him as my Man Friday, for in time I would increasingly start relying on him for routine and not so routine jobs. And yes! The buns, biscuits, and cakes that he would time and again dish out from his closet were a delight for the taste buds.

There was one problem, though… he couldn't speak a single word in English and I didn't know Arabic.

He did know how to pronounce 'passport,' which from his mouth seemed an Arabic word rather than English one. But, the fact of the matter was even the modest 'thank you' was alien to him, till I introduced it.

Frankly, hadn't it been for Messers Larry Page and Sergey Brin, we would have been groping in the dark.

Needless to say, Sajeer, the office boy from Kerala, who had been living in Doha for the last seven years and his co-workers, would often come to my aid during demanding situations of the 'linguistic kind'. And later when we moved office my colleague, Mahmoud, would do that job for us.

Often Nasir, another office-boy from the same Indian state as Sajeer, for whom Arabic was a second language, considering that he had been living in Qatar since the time his facial hair could be counted on fingers, would often double up as an interpreter for me.

The sound of the footsteps got heavier. The drag was akin to a heavily-built man lumbering his way up the hallway.

"*As-Salaam-Alaikum!*" With the deep baritone voice, Mustafa announced his presence and made his way into the room.

The man looked a bit under the weather. After all, he wasn't wearing his usual shirt, trousers and the trademark tie, but had instead adorned a *thob*. With great effort, he settled in his chair. And no sooner had his puffing and panting subsided that my name laced with a generous, albeit mispronounced dose of phonetics, reverberated across the large room.

The "Anaaam!" left me startled.

The exaggerated accentuation would have looked better in my school report card, especially of a certain English teacher, who would pronounce my name as if it were an airliner. The words "An Am" off her lips were music to my ears. A pat on the back and the frequent praise would often throw me into a tailspin of adolescent infatuation, traces of which still remain embedded in my subconscious.

In Mustafa's case, whoever, those extra 'As' were merely a sign of twist in linguistics or it could have been on account of his hearing aid, which he would take out when using the mobile phone and then forget to wear them.

The second time "Anaaam!" was accompanied by a hand gesture. I wondered, "What on earth is this man trying to say?"

Trying not to look agitated, I headed towards his desk. Abruptly, he said: "Google!" and launched the Google Translate window.

He typed in the words in the Arabic and soon the translation was there for me to decipher.

"It is important that you've got Petkdbna by saying I am Jet Lite door is open Then Ptaala voice very high and I Lesa in the new day and the morning I am a very normal as possible Forget Wi-installed so one possible But on the morning not fanatic."

A laughing stock that we had become, Mubarak was clearly in splits during one of his visits. But, a question from a Qatari colleague, who worked in the accounts department, more than summed up our situation.

"Google Translate, Man! Is it that bad?"

"Yes!" was all I could say.

Mustafa gives a thumbs up to Google Translate.

--x--

CONSERVATIVE, *NAH*!

I t was rather late. We were glued to the idiot box even as my mother was busy serving freshly baked *rotis* for dinner.

If memory serves me right it must have been the winter of 1989 or early 1990; I and brother, Khurram, were still in school. My father, a broadcast journalist, had developed a certain fondness for 'parallel cinema'.

In those days, in keeping with the changing times, the public broadcaster, Doordarshan, was busy experimenting with new wave cinema. Indian directors and producers were specially hired to produce films for the small screen. Also, European films of the arty sort found their way into the Indian living room.

I still vividly remember watching the much-acclaimed *Hanna K.,* by Greek French film director and producer

Costa-Gavras that intriguingly portrayed the intervening lives of the common folk caught in the midst of the Israel-Palestine conflict. The plot revolved around Hanna Kaufman, an American-Jewish lawyer in Israel, who is appointed to defend Salim Bakri, a Palestinian accused of terrorism.

The movie left an indelible mark on my young mind, accelerating my adolescence by months, if not by years.

On such an evening, an eastern European film was being aired on the telly. Just when I was about to gobble up the last morsel, I almost choked, not because I was eating too fast, but something just showed up on television that, if I may say, wasn't supposed to be for 'family audience'. What was worse was that the *damn* remote seemed to have vanished into thin air. By the time Khurram managed to locate it, the scene had become history. Luckily, the parents were not present at the scene of the crime.

As I sat in my hotel room watching Lebanese pop singer Layla Iskandar dish out her latest *'Maghourin'*, I couldn't stop wondering if the Middle East was witnessing a cultural revolution similar to the kind that had left me agape as a school kid.

"Now that certainly isn't conservative," I thought, awestruck by her chic image and loads of oomph.

A conversation with an Egyptian steward at the hotel only reinforced my belief that the Arabs certainly cannot be compartmentalised into what some western scribes call 'conservative'.

"Sir, you got to see them to believe me. Do check out Haifa Wehbe on the Google and you'd know," he said, referring to her spunk with special reference to Lebanon.

He was spot on, for more than her songs, which were a treat for the eyes (oops ears!); her passionate lip-locks on YouTube caught my attention. I was told that she wasn't just an avid singer, but her acting talent was 'phenomenal', which I could make out from the searches.

"Now that certainly isn't conservative,"
I thought, awestruck

Later, Adel Fateh would suggest me another name that would make me take on Google in a major way.

The Palestine-born, India-studied, Jordanian resident, who held a Canadian passport, was on a lookout for a job in Qatar.

17

I had met the 'universal citizen' at the hotel's spa and had instantly hit it off, with Nagpur being the common thread. The small, but centrally located Indian city was home to my father as a student. Years later Adel was to get admission in one of the colleges there.

Often we would go out for *sheesha*, or hookah as we say in India, at the cheap but chic Halul Café on Doha port. It was on his suggestion that I had searched for Nancy Ajram.

The beautiful 'Arab Idol' judge too turned out to be a Lebanese. No wonder, she was popular in this part of the world for her songs, *'Ma TegiHena'*, *'Fi Hagat'* and *'Ma Aw'edak Ma Gheer'*, which were utterly and completely mesmerising. This despite the fact that Arabic to me was what English was to my colleague Mustafa!

Closer home (by now Doha had become one for me) it didn't take me long before I had discovered the name 'Dana Alfardan'. The daughter of Qatari billionaire and business magnet, Hussain Ibrahim Alfardan, wasn't just busy charting out her course as a powerful business figure but, her debut album as a singer was well received.

The soulful English tracks of *'Paint'* with music to the match, had takers in the West as well. Later, she turned composer and went on to promote local talent. Here too she struck gold with *'Sandstorm'*. A 'difficult genre' as she described it, too struck a chord with the who's who of music.

I was trying to absorb the cultural scene of the landscape with music acting as a pivot for I wasn't exposed to cinema yet, with the language being a major hindrance, I couldn't stop myself from being taken over by Saudi singer and composer Mohammed Abdu's finesse.

'The Artist of Arabs' made me loathe myself for not knowing Arabic. His songs encompassing Arabic tradition had clearly stood the test of time. "Leave it, you won't be able to afford it," Adel had remarked seeing me holding a flier announcing his concert, during one of our visits to Katara.

I may have missed out on Abdu, but I didn't let the 'Caesar' get away. Iraqi's Kadim Al Sahir was a cynosure of all eyes, including mine, during the 24th Men's Handball Championships. Dubbed 'Caesar of Arabic Song', Kadim's voice calmed my senses that had been rendered taut following the pulsating action on the court.

Classical or pop, both genres had their unique influence on the Middle East map and that's how they influenced me – with their uniqueness. The *New York Times* report announcing the demise of the famous Morteza Pashaei summed up the emotions with a screaming heading: *"Public Grieving for Pop Singer Is Startling for Iran"*.

Pashaei, 30, who died of stomach cancer, was so popular a figure that the authorities had trouble controlling the mourners, who had swelled up in numbers at his funeral. This despite the fact, that many of his songs were banned from the state television in Iran because they were 'too romantic'.

Such is the sway of music – tougher the restrictions, the farther it spreads.

"This should surprise you," I had told Adel, once. "I had a taste of Arabic songs as a kid."

"That's interesting! How so?"

"Khaled's *'Didi'* was my all-time favourite then," I remarked.

I have to admit that I had taken to Wikipedia to learn about Qatar before I started my Doha sojourn. And the line, "After Saudi Arabia, Qatar is the most conservative society in the GCC..." did leave me a bundle of nerves, which, were left undone upon arrival, much like Layla undid her stitched lips and later her garb in *'Maghourin'*.

--x--

THE SMÖRGÅSBORD

His chiselled physique could have put to shame those home shopping models selling 'ab pro' machines on the telly.

Considering his abs, the little bulge around my bellybutton was a picture, in contrast, ideal for a company selling slimming equipment with me standing in the middle of the spectrum. Yes! Manoj, the young man from Punjab and I, like the rest of them, stood there topless.

No! It wasn't a spa, nor was it a destination for orgies or any such place that would have raised eyebrows or would have put a question mark in the minds of the guardians of the ethics. We were at the Medical Commission getting ready for the X-ray. Together with the blood test, it constituted the medical test – a prerequisite in Qatar.

There was little I could do other than watch men in their varied degree of semi-nudity. Some potbellied, others putting their abs to good display, yet others competing for the 'most toned bicep title' with their smart phones coming in handy.

Even as I got ready to expand my chest in a room devoid of light, I couldn't stop but notice that the place was actually a melting pot of cultures, much like that dartboard with the map of the world pasted on it. Spot the country where the dart lands and for certain its people would be present in this country spanning just 4,468 square miles.

Qatar came to me like a smörgåsbord, with its nooks, corners and even those modest bus stops displaying the unique characteristic of that Scandinavian meal with dozens of hot and cold dishes thrown open to an expert connoisseur.

"Sir, you need to wear proper gym shoes," he had said, pointing towards my boots, which were creating an odd stomping sound on the treadmill. Wazeem Cammar, the well-built gym instructor, sounded stern.

His drop-dead looks that accentuated the 'stern quotient' made a rebel like me fall in line. I was so taken aback by his sudden interjection, that from then on his very presence in the gym would make me perform a hasty exit. This would have carried on for days until a certain Rohit Sharma hit 264 against Sri Lanka and I couldn't help but sit back at the reception and read the entire sports page of a local daily rather than visiting the treadmill or the pool.

Seeing me engrossed with those reports, he couldn't stop himself. "I saw that match. He was simply brilliant."

"Oh, you did. I am sure he must have."

"I mean the guy hit a whopping 33 fours in it. Looks like a massive thumping," I had said. Sarcasm was dripping from my tone.

He made light of the matter, and cricket ate up a large chunk of our conversation. Soon enough it became a trend with both of us gelling over the gentleman's game.

That day was different. Wazeem must have been in a retrospective mood, making me realise that the tall Sri Lankan had already passed through the 'been there, done that' phase in life. The man who would hobnob with the likes of B-Town star Jacqueline Fernandez and was on the cusp of stardom with the coveted Mr. Sri Lanka title under his belt was forced to lead a life of unqualified penury.

All was lost in a flash.

"I won the crown in 2012 and the World title was up for the grabs," said the islander.

"But, there was no chance that I could have funded it. Our financial situation had gone down from bad to worse," he lamented.

"Around the same time this offer came about and I took it up. I didn't have a choice. I was the only earning member in my family then."

"But did you approach any external agencies or sponsors?" I had asked.

"Sir, being in Sri Lanka it is a difficult thing to do. Had I been to London, I would have been among the who's who of the modelling circuit."

He had reasons to feel that way, after all, the man not just fitted precisely into the 'tall, dark handsome' bracket, but was the face of many a high-end brands till he was forced into the wilderness at a young age of 26.

Wazeem may have missed the opportunity, but his eyes still had that unmistakable glint that spoke of his undaunted resolve. The determination that lets a man pursue his dreams, come what may.

"By the way, I am not the only one with riches to rags story at this hotel. Go down to the front office and you'd come across another one."

"Oh yes! I have heard of that one. Let me see if it's her shift today," I said, packing my gear.

A quick shower and I were already walking down the ground floor hallway.

At the front office, Wazeem's colleague Audrey Choge was busy welcoming the guests. Every now and then she would sport that captivating smile until finally it came my way.

The young Kenyan had been working at Doha Downtown for close to two years now. Her story, though, vastly different from Wazeem had its share of stardom.

But, unlike the model turned gym-instructor, it was an adventure that had brought the former actress to Doha.

"I wanted to travel, so here I am doing just that," said Audrey, whose movie *'Keeping It Together'* was amongst the 'Top 10' Kenyan movies in 2012. Another titled *'LOVE, Taken to a mysterious place'* was well appreciated. But life had other plans for her, as was evident from her choices in life.

Was the student of hospitality management keen on putting her education to good use or was she justifying the move, only her heart would know the answer, for Audrey could have hit the zenith of showbiz or was already there before she was besieged by the desire to travel. So overwhelmed was she, that even a sedentary job offer from a hotel in Doha looked irresistible.

"One day I might just go back to acting. I really want to act alongside Shah Rukh Khan," added the starry-eyed receptionist.

Her naivety caught me unawares. "Did she say, Shah Rukh Khan?"

Even though I wanted to say that stars like him don't act with just about anyone, all I could utter were "You are aware that he is a billionaire?"

"Yes! I am aware. But, what's that got to do with acting," she quipped. I was left speechless.

Elsewhere, Adel sat glaring into the void even as the drags from his *sheesha* filled the air with smoke.

"Way back in 1996, there was just a small six-storied building, other than that," he said, pointing towards the majestic boat-shaped Sheraton Hotel on the West Bay.

Adel, the unique character that he was, had sacrificed his entire life on the altar to relocate to the Arabian Gulf. This, too, after obtaining a Canadian passport – a much sought after 'document' by many. Countless Indians marry off their daughters to expatriates based in Canada so that they get to lead a good and prosperous life. But, here was a man, who was born in the war-torn state of Palestine, and had spent donkey number of years in Canada only to call it a day, baffled me.

"Why would one do it?" I wondered.

Even more striking was the fact that he had separated from his wife of 22 years because she had resisted the relocation plan.

It sure does make sense if one plans for a quiet retirement, but clearly he hadn't. Adel not only decided to move to Jordan but also took a second wife, a Syrian.

So now Adel has two wives and three kids, two in colleges from the first one and one just three months old from the second.

The story doesn't end there for Adel who now lives in Jordon, decided to come to Qatar to look for a job and used up his savings staying the same starred hotel that I was staying in.

"Nobody does that, Adel! No wonder your wife decided to stay back in Canada," I said, trying to reason with him. "Yes, but a wife should follow her husband wherever he goes." His words reeked of patriarchy.

Perchance, he wanted to try his luck once again in the same desert that had bestowed him with riches before he had moved to ice-capped hills.

Adel probably would never have made me understand what Qatar had meant for him, but 20-something Tirupati, the housekeeping attendant at the office had hit the nail on the head when he said, "I like it here." His words carried more weight when I came to know that he was seriously ill.

Tirupati had diabetes and was forced to take insulin injections twice every day to keep his sugar levels under check.

"I like it here…." The words were reverberating in my mind when the "NEXT!" gate-crashed the door of my thoughts.

I walked in, stood next to the X-ray machine, held my breath and it was over before I could comprehend.

As I went out of the glass door, I couldn't help, but ask the guard, "That's it! Can I go to the office now?"

"Yes Sir! That's it," he replied. "Office, well… you can go anywhere you like, *Habibi*!"

As I was about to leave, I noticed another line close to the door that read: "Toilet".

"Oh! Did I forget the urine test," wondering I stepped closer to investigate, only to be greeted with guffaws. "No, no… it's not that," said a man suggestively.

Smiling at my foolhardiness, I walked away.

The man had not only quit his job, but was home amongst the glitterati of the fashion industry.

Months later, Wazeem's Facebook page got me hooked. Pictures of him walking the ramp were flooded with likes. I would have dismissed them as old. But, for those words that made me reconsider.

"At Moratuwa University show. After 3years… back to RAMP," the post read.

Later, a chat with him revealed that the man had not only quit his job, but was home amongst the glitterati of the fashion industry. Precisely why I hadn't seen him for days.

"It was by chance that I had met one of my choreographers and that set the ball rolling," he told me.

--x--

LIVE AND LET PLAY

He let the water from the tap clear the dirt off his feet. The ablution was slow. It was supposed to be that way, but his hands slowed down as they reached for the toe. The blood clot under the toenail had turned it black.

The fingers went nimble, lest they should cause any agony. For a second my eyes could not see anything, but that blackened toenail. I knew there was a story behind it.

Post the *Namaz*, I couldn't help but ask, "Do you play football?"

"Ah!" He got a shock of life. "How do you know?"

I just smiled, heightening his curiosity.

"*Bhai*! You seem to know everything," he had said.

Later, while serving coffee, he looked anxiously at me.

"What is it?" I asked and signalled him the chair, which he grabbed quickly, and removing his boots, revealed the pink crape bandage.

He was a footballer, after all.

No wonder, he loved to display his wounds like that of a soldier. His battlefield was different, though. An unkempt patch of a land with a heterogeneous mixture of grass, sand and gravel in Madinat Khalifa, bore witness to his footballing exploits.

"See *bhai*, I got this injury yesterday evening." The glint in the eye was enough to hide his pain.

"He just charged at me and struck after I had patted the ball into the net. There wasn't any reason, still he kicked my ankle," he pointed out.

"But how do you know about the toenail?"

"I have been struck by that problem too," I explained.

"So, did you play too?"

"Yes, very briefly and it was because of those boots. That's why when I saw your toenail, I knew you were a footballer too," I added.

Nasir, 32, had entered into the wedlock more than a decade ago. A father to three, he was to spend only a few months with his family in a nondescript village in Kerala, before the long-drawn Middle East sojourn started for the young man.

But, the man was driven by football.

"Oh! I have been playing since the time I actually learnt to stand," he would boast.

In a way, he wasn't wrong. After all, he had only started playing when he came to Doha. And, it was around that very time, he had learnt to stand on his feet, financially speaking.

And, no sooner were his financial wherewithal addressed, he got on with what he loved the most. So engrossed, would he be in the game, that he would push his sleep by hours together.

"I don't sleep much."

"Can you imagine I come back at 12 in the night," he had said while driving me home from work.

"But why would you do that," I asked genuinely concerned.

"*Bhai*, I enjoy playing," was the simple reply.

Simple it was, but it summed up the entire world for a sports aficionado.

It was that very adrenaline rush that made me cling to my job like a leech, drawing energy from the friction that goes on the field. And, even though I had been virtually reduced to being an 'armchair aficionado', it didn't stop me from pushing my limits, especially during those high-octane games.

I may have missed the Paris Saint-Germain vs Inter Milan friendly, thanks to my lazy attribution, which saw me apply for the accreditation rather late. But, there definitely is one match, which has been wired up my intellectual server forever.

The adrenaline charge was there, only the outlet was missing.

It was cold that evening and warm water in the pool after a hard day's work was inviting. I shed my clothes, took a towel and with my boxers doubling up as swimwear, I let the water do magic on my tired muscles.

A single thrust and I were in the deep, touching the bottom of the 4-feet pool, designed for recreation rather than sport.

Downstairs, Town Café, the restaurant, was engulfed in stale smoke and the aroma of strong Turkish coffee. Gigantic TV sets installed in each corner had started attracting a large audience.

The commotion was understood, in fact, it was an understatement considering that Serie A giants Juventus and Napoli were lining up for a faceoff a quarter of notch away, at the Jassim Bin Hamad Stadium in the vicinity.

It was the Supercoppa Italiana!

I had asked the attendant to turn on the TV, as I headed for the area that housed the Jacuzzi. Cursing my luck, I would have settled for 'second-hand excitement' like the rest of them at the restaurant, but for that phone call.

I tripped on the wet floor, but still managed to hold on to the phone. I tapped the green button, without glancing at the name; the fall had left me dazed.

"Hi," said the familiar voice. Without a doubt, it was Mubarak on the line.

"Hi," he repeated and went on, "I have got the tickets for the match."

The attendant, who had rushed to my aid, was expecting the cliché 'oh!', 'ah!' or an 'ouch!', but a "wow" off my lips was definitely not what she had expected.

With an "Ah, I am good!" I got up and wobbled off towards the changing room. A healthy dab of the Tiger Balm on the hurting knee and I was out on the road, frantically gesturing the taxis to stop.

"Too much traffic there." The blatantly blunt driver drove past in a jiffy.

Ten minutes on the pavement, with my patience running an all-time low, I decided to walk.

But, it seemed lady luck was smiling on me that day. Seconds later another one pulled up along the curb and this time, the driver wasn't aware of the traffic snarls caused by the much-awaited game.

With, the meter up and running, the evil in me raised its ugly head and I decided to let the Nepalese driver get a feel of the impending traffic scenario.

My update about the big game left him disoriented, making him look for excuses to drop me off, and midway through the journey. But, I was hardly in a mood to relent and stayed on, enjoying the changing contours of his face. Clearly, the man was cursing me.

I got off near the ticketing counter, which was still crowded with those latecomers wishing to make an entry. After a few hasty phone calls, I managed to locate Mubarak.

Dressed in a dark *thob*, in keeping with the changing season, he looked chic. I spotted him on the far side of the counter waving towards me. Quickly I rushed towards him and within minutes we were in.

By the time we entered, Argentine legend Carlos Tevez had already put one in, and Napoli were busy playing catch-up. From the looks of it, Juve were content in letting their famed defence consisting of big names like Giorgio Chiellini, Leonardo Bonucci, Stephan Lichtsteiner and Patrice Evra do the talking.

As the match continued, I came to know that Mubarak was a Napoli fan and he had predicted their victory. I, on the other hand, was supporting the Old Lady, another name for Juventus.

My fondness for them dates back to my days spent at *Hindustan Times*. It was then, that I was made to endure monologues from a colleague in support of the Serie A giants. Sadly, for that diehard Juve fan, it was the same year they were relegated to Serie B.

Call it a blessing in disguise, the Turin club, which was forced to play at lesser-known grounds, used the opportunity to connect with its fans in far-flung areas. They bounced back, as was expected, and in the process struck a chord in my heart.

It must have been long before Napoli equalised with Tevez's countryman Gonzalo Higuain's scoring his first goal in seven games. The first half got over with scores levelled 1-1.

The break gave us time to grab a bite and even discuss our varied interests in sports. That's when Mubarak told me how his interests in football had grown over the ages.

"My father was a big fan of Napoli," he had said.

"I should have guessed. Admiration does tend to flow across generations."

"That's correct, but we would also watch other big games," he said, narrating an incident from a World Cup encounter, post which he was practically eating, sleeping, and drinking football.

The second half proved to be rather tame with the two Argentine stars performing an encore. Extra time too failed to break the deadlock. And just when I was beginning to think Mubarak's assumption was wrong; Napoli came out in flying colours, holding aloft the silverware amidst much fanfare and confetti.

The night had ended, but the excitement lingered on. But, it wasn't the biggest of occasions for me, which is far. After all, it has been earmarked for 2022.

So, here I am waiting for that biggest footballing extravaganza while Nasir is busy nursing his toenail. On the field, however, he is in the running for the Most Valuable Player of a tournament for the third year in a row...

--x--

FROM ECSTASY TO AGONY

The din was completely and utterly overpowering.

A beeline of cars carrying replicas of the national flag had converged at the West Bay. Qatar had defeated Saudi Arabia in the final of the Arabian Gulf Cup at the latter's backyard in Riyadh – reason enough for everyone to celebrate. Citizens, residents, and visitors were busy honking their horns to mark the historic win, which had eluded them for a decade.

Adel and I were at our usual hangout, the Halul Café, taking turns with the *sheesha* even as the 'cavalcade' of cars carrying revellers, passed by. Some dressed in the teams colours, others waving the flags, others honking – it definitely was one of a kind experience.

We had been watching for an hour when I sensed that something was amiss. "Where are the drums, man?" I asked even as I watched the procession go by.

"Oh, they don't need that. Those horns are enough," said Adel, looking somewhat puzzled at my sudden interjection.

Adel and I were at our usual hangout, the Halul Café, taking turns with the sheesha.

Memories from an old football match that I had covered in New Delhi flashed by.

It was the 2003-04 Santosh Trophy final between Kerala and Punjab. Back then, I worked as a reporter for *The Asian Age*, probably the only newspaper in India that has dedicated readers in England, owing to its London edition. Unfortunately, for us, that 'edition' was made in New Delhi.

So, all my reporting assignments were usually followed by a gruelling exercise called 'page making.' We had nicknamed it '*dabba* (box) making' for the number of text boxes that had to be made using page-making software, QuarkXPress, which was the medium for bonded labour then. These days they call those 'shackles' InDesign.

That day, the match had stretched into extra time with Kerala winning on golden goal and I had just enough time to file the story and not worry about page-making. But, of course, a '*dabba*' had been designated for my story.

No sooner had the match got over that hordes of Kerala fans, wearing the *mundu* (traditional outfit), were out there on the pitch with *chenda* (wooden drum) hanging from their necks. I am not too sure if they were paid to play there, but their vigorous drumming had pulled just about every spectator off the seat and into the pitch.

The ambience was so arresting that had I not got that call, I would have stayed there for hours. I tore myself from the place and rushed to catch a bus for the office, where 'music of a different kind' awaited my ears...

I may not have chanced upon the drums at West Bay that night, but they certainly have their significance as I was to discover later.

Meanwhile, Al Corniche looked more like a venue for the gala event, rather than just being a waterfront promenade lined with palm trees. The revellers were there as far as my eye could see.

Their high-pitched honking reminded me of the 2010 FIFA World Cup in South Africa with images of fans blowing the '*vuvuzela*' splashed all over the newsprint.

It was as if I were sitting in a stadium packed with fans playing the noisy instrument, except that the deafening sounds were automated. They were far from the type of celebrations that are witnessed in European or Latin American soccer, where the exaggerated display of emotions and gestures are a cliché.

"That's because there's no alcohol here," said Adel, as if reading my mind.

"Did I say anything about liquor?"

"But, it does lead to unruliness," he added.

"I am not sure if you have heard about the 'Hillsborough disaster'."

He looked at me. The question mark was writ large across his face.

"In 1989, the Liverpool and Nottingham Forest match at Hillsborough Stadium was so jam-packed that there was a stampede."

"As many as 96 people died there," I said.

For decades, the world was made to believe that unruly fan behaviour led to the disaster until it emerged that serious administrative lapses caused it.

I would have said more but, my voice drowned under the cacophony of horns, which had reached a new high on decibels.

The temporary 'Carmageddon' had brought to halt the entire traffic at the West Bay.

That evening too Adel had parked his car near the curb adjoining the Café. The crowd had swelled by the time we decided to exit. "What the hell!" said Adel, trying to make himself audible above the din. "It's just too crowded today."

A good driver that he was, he quickly managed to trace a way past the stream of cars.

"Now that we are out of this mess, what do you suggest?"

"Let's get on with some sightseeing," he said, and moments later was driving towards the nearby Souq Waqif. Though I should have guessed that a particular Turkish delicacy was high on his priority list, which I soon discovered.

Souq Waqif or the "standing market" is an excellent shopping destination situated in the heart of Doha. As New Delhi's Connaught Place, it has stood the test of time for more than a century, but, still has its charms intact.

A delight for the connoisseurs of art, the refurbished shopping destination is lined with shops selling traditional garments, spices, handicrafts, and souvenirs. Items so mesmerising that they would leave an impulsive buyer's wallet burnt to shards, forget about the hole in the pocket scenario. For us, window shoppers, however, it definitely was a remarkable place. After all, our pockets weren't loaded enough to witness any such attack of the monetary nature.

Then again, we were not even inside the Gold Souq – that 'yellow sea' which could drain the mega rich dry. Fortunately, both Adel and I happened to be good swimmers. We knew just when to pop our heads out for a breather, in other words, be awed and step out with a "Thank you!" on our lips.

We didn't use the breather technique too often, though, it should become a cliché. At times, we would step inside the shop posing as happy customers, check out the prices, which obviously were jaw-dropping. We wouldn't let our jaws perform that act and instead get engaged in vivid conversations, make faces, and towards the end of the 'act' nobly step out.

I did succumb to the pleasures of the yellow metal, but at a later date when I was heading home during my annual leave. At that moment, however, I was just happy to see those poor men shell out their hard earned *moolah* to appease their beautiful WAGs – not an unusual feature considering that gold prices have always been cheaper in this part of the world. No wonder that women from the subcontinent start eyeing their husband's wallet upon arrival in the Arabian Gulf.

What actually caught my attention was the bird market or the Bird Souq where Falcons sat quietly on wooden perches or the hands of their owners, other held aloft by the visitors desirous of a click or two. Had they not occasionally bobbed their heads, I would have thought them to be of plastic, such was their composure.

Tamed, with their eyes covered with leather hoods, the creatures are a prized possession in the Middle East. Their importance in the region can be gauged from the fact that many countries including Qatar have the image of the bird printed on currency notes.

In fact, the other day at work, Mubarak had shown me a picture where he was seen posing with the beast perched on his arm.

To a Falcon connoisseur, the place is an absolute delight for it's a one stop destination for all his needs of the 'bird kind'. Loaded with shops selling paraphernalia like leather hoods, gloves, landing pads and so also the high-tech GPS guiding system, it definitely was worth a visit.

A little research had told me that Falcons are rather expensive creatures, much in demand during the month-long falconry festival, when their prices soar to an eye-popping 400,000 Riyals. Also, catching and breeding the Falcon is an art in itself. Renowned British author, the late Edward Henderson portrayed the intricacies of the job in great detail in his autobiography – *'Arabian Destiny'*.

The unique 'Falcon Hospital' in close quarters, dedicated for the treatment of the large birds, took me by surprise. But then, if a person is willing to shell millions for the bird, he definitely would be eager to keep it fit.

I would have ventured further, had Adel not spotted that Turkish Restaurant, popular among the diners for its *'Shawarma'*.

The *Shawarma* or *Shawurma* as it is often called is a Turkish delicacy where an assortment of meats (usually from lamb, chicken, turkey, and beef) is placed on a vertical skewer and heated. Shavings are cut off the block and served on a platter or a *Khubus* (Arabian pita bread) wrap with toppings made of lettuce, tomatoes, coriander leaves and a bit of olive oil adding to the richness of the taste.

So that was our plan for the night –impeccably cooked *Shawarma* topped with an animated discussion. Adding to the ambience was the strong aroma of Turkish coffee and the very popular *Sulaimani* tea (red or black tea) with mint.

The morning after, I headed for the lobby to check out the local dallies.

They all were filled with images, reports, and analysis of how Qatar had humbled Saudi Arabia. It was as if young David had humbled the mighty Goliath.

"Kings of Gulf Football" screamed the lead headline of a local daily. I flipped the paper wanting to see more reports from the same match, but a news agency report

"Australia's Hughes continues to fight for life" snatched the smile away from my face.

Phillip Hughes, 25, succumbed to his head injury, and my ecstasy turned into agony within seconds.

--x--

THE WEDDING AFFAIR

I was fashionably late, but instead of feeling ashamed, openly flaunted the fact.

"I have been coming late these days," I said, with a sense of misplaced pride, which should have been put to a test. But Mubarak didn't question my commitment towards work and just asked, "Why?"

Perhaps, both of us knew the answer, but we chose not to discuss the 'Achilles heel' of Qatar… or were it mine, I am still undecided on that front. But, the subconscious mind tried to justify it, putting a bizarre logic to it, rather than talking about the 'usual' transport or traffic issues.

The uncanny rationality, though an oxymoron, was that only efficient and intelligent people come late as they are able to do the same amount of work in lesser time than those, who are punctual. Now, I don't intend to patronise the latecomers or let down the early birds but, the fact is, the latter has little rewards. Probably, the best and the most well-known is that no one is around to appreciate it.

Ironically, this odd logic was presented to me by one of my former bosses, who too knew that I was a chronic latecomer. But, I am definitely not falling into that trap and I would just say that punctuality is vital for efficiency and that's precisely why I had decided to apply for the 'coveted' driving licence.

Maybe, Mubarak wasn't too concerned about my late coming as there was something else on his mind and I learnt about it soon enough. He had a bunch of invitation cards for a family wedding. Needless to say, I was invited and what's more, I could bring a friend along. That obviously would have meant that Adel was to accompany me to the venue.

The next day, he was ready to go. Sadly, I wasn't. I was still on my way back to hotel post work and somehow it took me longer than the usual. The traffic restrictions surrounding the National Day preparations would have added to the delay, but they certainly didn't ruin my plans for the evening.

It must have been past 9 when we reached the Diplomatic Club in Katara. A well-lit *shamiyana* (tent) with an all-male gathering beckoned us. It was Mubarak's nephew's wedding.

Though he was busy with the guests, Mubarak found time to meet us and even introduced us to the groom Khalid and his father Mohammed Al Boainin. Dressed in a chic *thob*, with a classy *bisht* (outer gown) on top, accompanied with a *keffiyeh* to match, the groom looked immaculate.

After facing the flash bulbs in the august company, we made ourselves comfortable on large king-size seats that reminded me of my wedding. After all, how often does one get that type of royal treatment? And it definitely was regal, as folk singers and indigenous dancers delighted us with their music and deft movements with swords in hand. The large drums acted as the icing on the cake.

Both, Adel and I got busy clicking pictures. Later, I got to know that ladies are not allowed to carry their smart camera phones in the women's section as this is one of those few occasions where an Arab woman lets her guard down and can be spotted in flamboyant and avant-garde designer wear. Though specialist women photographers are specifically hired for the job, but they are given a clear mandate where to focus and where not to.

Soon it was time for the buffet and being a foodie, I was looking forward to a great dining experience. Hence, I steered clear of the juices, sodas, and other liquids and headed for the hard-core stuff.

*Indigenous dancers delighted us with their music
and deft movements with swords in hand.*

The very popular *Machboos,* a rice-based dish with a
unique blend of spices and meat, was certainly there and
so was the *Margoog.*

The most striking part about *Margoog* is that is uses
raw bread dough. The dough is kneaded for hours making
it extremely soft. It is then cut into stripes or pieces and
then boiled into a stock of liquid that is saturated with
concentrated vegetable and meat. The process soaks
up all that savoury goodness turning it into a mouth-
watering delicacy. Not to forget, there were other spices
and ingredients playing their respective part and I let my
taste buds play a judge to them.

Delicacies from Yemeni haute cuisine too had made its way on to my plate with *Mandi* and *Saltah* turning me into a connoisseur of fine Arabian foods.

And for those having a sweet tooth, the flavours of *Baklava and Kunafa*, that owe their presence to the Ottoman Turks and the *Umm Ali,* from the land of the Sphinx, had made my evening 'mouth-watering'.

Much like those famed wine tasters, I would pick extremely small quantities of each and would leisurely consume them. As a result, I was among the first to enter the dining zone and the last one to exit. As luck would have it, those happy moments were short-lived and soon it was time to bid adieu.

A parting handshake and we were on the road, caught in the 'warp drive' of thoughts. The monosyllables running through my mind would have pushed me to the brink of dreaming, but for those untimely words, "Hey, you know what!" denied me those moments of most basic leisure."

"What... what... what the..."

"Wake up, you should know this," he said, mischievously.

"Oh, man...." I would have cursed him, but instead said: "Shoot!"

"Marriage customs can be really, really weird," he said.

"No! Not again," I thought. I was hardly in a mood to listen to another of his exploits of distant lands. After all, they can be really disconcerting following a sumptuous meal.

Still, I gave him my ears, even though the eyes must have been busy blinking.

"You know how old my second wife is," he asked, playfully.

"How does that concern me, Adel?"

"She's 34!" A smile played on his lips.

An array of expletives rushed through my mind, but opted for a modest, "Ah ha, Lucky you."

"My wife's father, a Syrian, was so possessive about his daughter that he couldn't stand the sight of her getting married and moving out," he said, even as he pushed the hand-break.

"The guy just wouldn't let her get married. In fact, he would send back all the prospective grooms."

"Okay! So how did a hideous old man like you, managed to get her?" I asked, surprised.

"I just got lucky. Besides, she too was adamant."

"But the man was very upset. Neither he, nor his sons showed up at the wedding."

I didn't pay much heed to his perceptions, got off, and headed towards the lift. In time, I was in the dreamland, after all.

--x--

Thank you, Steve Jobs!

My woes concerning the daily commute had somewhat subsided. The reason was a Malaysian fellow, whom I had met while returning from office the other day.

I gathered that he lived in Al Sadd and worked in Dafna, the two destinations around which my home (read hotel) and work life revolved.

Soon, Eric and I were sharing a drive to the office – a more convenient and efficient method compared to taking a bus from Al Sadd to Doha Station for a change to Al Corniche or Dafna, as it's popularly called.

Initially, we started flagging the Karwa taxies, but within a couple of days Eric had managed to locate a limousine driver, who agreed to hitch us a drive for 20 Riyals with Eric and I splitting the cost.

It was a routine Tuesday morning, the 'iPhone 6 Plus' alarm went off at 5:45 am, followed by those precious minutes of snooze before I quickly took a shower, performed the mundane chores, picked up the apple (read breakfast) and rushed to catch the taxi.

All three of us chatted on our way to Dafna, and we even planned out a Friday breakfast outing at the nearby South Indian restaurant that offered appetising delicacies, ranging from *Dosa, Wada, Uthappam, Sambhar* and the humble *Idli*, which though mouth-watering, are rather light on the stomach.

Uthayan, the Sri Lankan driver, who had been living in Qatar for the last 15 years and could speak fluent Hindi, English, and Arabic, dropped Eric at the Salaam tower a few blocks away before turning around for my destination - the Olympic Tower.

As it was a habit, I checked the contents of my bag, only to make sure I hadn't left anything behind.

Even as my hands fiddled around the files and pockets of my bag, I was shocked to realise that my phone had gone amiss.

And, before I could wave to Uthayan to stop, he was out of sight – a natural phenomenon considering that the speed limit in most areas in Doha is above 80 km/hr.

Shocked and shaken, I realised that I only had Eric's number and not Uthayan's. And that too was saved in the phone memory and not the one that resided in my cranium.

I rushed towards the Salaam Tower without even analysing the fact that I did not know where Eric worked. And it was rather tough to locate one Malaysian expat in a building that housed hundreds of offices and showrooms. It was akin to locating a needle in a haystack. Even more troublesome was the fact that Tower houses four sub-towers.

I looked around trying to locate Eric. That was when someone suggested that I try out the Malaysian Trade Centre on the fourth floor. I reached there only to be told that the office opens at 9:00 am.

Back on the ground floor, I approached two Nepalese cleaners, who suggested the obvious. "Did you try calling your own phone," said one.

That sentence made me reflect upon, how stupid and naïve I had been all this while. I could have simply gone to my office and dialled my own phone, end of story. Instead, I had tried the weirdest methods for locating it. Maybe, the anxiety had left me deranged.

Quickly, I grabbed his phone and dialled my number to be greeted by an automated feminine voice in Arabic, followed by one in English informing me that the 'person I was trying to reach was unavailable'.

"Obviously, I was unavailable to answer that call," I thought, irritation drawn across my face.

Repeated attempts came to nought with virtually no response from the other end. Later, the feminine voice told me that my phone was switched off. My heart sank.

That's when the other cleaner suggested that I approach the police. So I just said, "Let me dial 999."

Scared, he snatched the phone and asked me to go to the place where the incident had happened, and check out the camera and get hold of the images and then approach the police – a rather long and weird process, which was clearly aimed at driving me off.

That's when I saw another Nepalese man using an iPhone. It must have been an iPhone 5. I knew that I could access the phone's contacts by using the iCloud facility. Unfortunately, he hadn't configured it, so the phone was pretty much useless. What was even worse was the fact that the man didn't know what iCloud was all about.

With a prayer on my lips, I made a hasty exit. As I passed the popular Lavazza coffee shop, I noticed a man, coffee in his hand, glued to his MacBook. With striking agility, I approached him and uttered, "I lost my iPhone".

Those four words were enough for the thorough nobleman to gauge my plight. "Oh!" he said and quickly vacated his seat for me. Within seconds, I had opened my iCloud inbox and located Eric's phone number.

Tension and anxiety had taken its toll. I dialled Eric's number using his handset, but couldn't reach him despite many attempts. That's when I requested him to use the WhatsApp Messenger. He tried, but even that didn't work and the service provider returned with the message: "the number is invalid". Frustrated and tensed, I was trying to figure out what to do next when my eyes fell on the number. A crosscheck made me realise that instead of dialling '6' towards the end, I had dialled '9'.

All this while, the Good Samaritan provided me with much-needed comfort saying, "Don't worry, you can locate your iPhone with the Find My iPhone facility."

"Nobody steals in Qatar," he said, and offered a reassurance with, "Not that I know of."

Eventually, I did manage to speak with Eric and also with Uthayan, who told me that I was lucky that on his way back, he didn't get any customers and so the phone was safe in his custody. His words were like music to my ears giving me instant relief.

"How about some coffee?" said, John S. Papaioannou, steering clear of the near catastrophic chain of events that had beseeched me seconds ago.

I thanked him, politely refusing the offer, but I could not resist a cigarette. "I don't smoke much, but now I just want to," I said and urged him for one.

"Yes, I know it's almost like sex. You do like to smoke after you have been relieved," he said jokingly and offered me one.

We had a quick chat, exchanged our numbers and that's when I came to know that John, a Greek, who had also lived in Canada and Bahrain, had recently moved to Doha and was in the process of setting up a restaurant in close quarters.

Christened 'JUSTINCASE', the restaurant was to offer mouth-watering Mediterranean delicacies.

"I am sure it would!" I thought and walked back.

That evening, Uthayan dropped by at the hotel and my prized possession was back to where it belonged –my pocket. That was the last I saw of the Islander, who currently resides in my Facebook contact list.

Eric, meanwhile, had decided to turn a chapter. The accountant, after making just enough money to settle his liabilities, returned home to his loving wife and daughter in Kuala Lumpur. And soon enough my commute issues came back to haunt me.

And JUSTINCASE does offer mouth-watering delicacies. Ask my taste buds… they don't lie.

--x--

Adel does a Houdini act

I returned to the hotel that evening after a hard day of commuting. For, it wasn't the work, but the daily commute that would leave me drained. To top it, what followed was shocking. The blatant use of my room by an undesired individual wasn't something I had expected.

Adel opened the door to a rather dark backdrop. It was obvious that he was catching up on his afternoon siesta. Man, I wondered, here I am the actual guest, who has been lodged up in the hotel for six months, but I am the one who is made to suffer even as this guy, who doesn't have a job, has two families to feed, and yet has enough time to catch up on his sleep.

I quickly performed the ablution, did the evening prayers and ordered for my regular cuppa along with some light snack.

"Would you like some," I asked out of courtesy, even though deep down I hoped that he uttered "Nah, no, or negative" or similar sounding words.

Frankly, the boredom had set in and I had begun to dislike his stay or overstay, which too was an understatement. For, like a leech he was sucking up my sparse resources. The dismay was so great that my hotel room seemed like an epicentre of theatrics with the age-old fable, 'The Arab and His Camel' being played out amidst loud applause. No points for guessing the who's who in the act.

The way he came into my life and later into my room was strikingly similar to the way the camel had entered his master's tent.

First, his clothes found their way into my closet. "I would be leaving for Jordan shortly. Is it possible for you to keep these suits?"

"Just let them hang there. I should be coming back in a month's time, no point in carrying them along," he had said.

"Why don't you leave it at your friend's," I said. Adel's friend from Palestine, who too had studied in Nagpur, was staying with his entire family at the hotel and since their friendship went back to the 'days of the yore', it wasn't an inappropriate suggestion.

"Ah! That would be difficult for him. You know he is a family man and his wife…."

"Okay, okay!" I knew what was coming up next, so even before he could complete the sentence, I gave in. Though, I visualised: *"Master, it's very cold outside. Please allow me to put my head inside your tent."*

And then the act was played out with much fanfare.

'Out of pity, the benevolent master agreed to the camel's request. A little later, the camel asked, "Master, please let me put my neck inside your tent as well." The master nodded in affirmative.

The camel then asked if he could put his forelegs in and again the master Okayed the request. Soon, the camel was completely inside the tent and the master was pushed out of the small tent and into the cold.'

Adel was turning out to be the very camel for me who had pushed his master out in the cold. But, before he could perform the trick on me I decided to show him the way to the door.

Also, that day he had almost crossed the limit...

I had made myself comfortable on the couch and was getting ready for my regular dosage from the television, when Adel pointed towards the packet on the table. "That should be for you!"

The packet contained the copy of the LPO (Local Purchase Order) along with room service invoices of the last couple of months. The same I was required to deposit at my office so that my outstanding dues could be settled.

I carefully went through the bills to check if I had overshot my limit for any particular day. Towards the end, I noticed peculiar signatures which spelt my name in the crudest possible manner. That was when it dawned on me that the man had actually signed my name.

"Oh My God," I yelled at the top of my voice.

"Adel, just what do you think you are up to?" I was furious. "This is plain, bland forgery in its blatant form."

"What could I do, the room service boy was standing there and looking at me in the face? Besides, it's not like what you perceive it to be. Oh come now, it's not a forgery," he went on the defensive.

"Okay! If that was the case then why didn't you sign your own name?"

"How could I do that? In that case, I would have had to pay for it," he said calmly.

"You can order food, but can't pay. Smart, very smart," I quipped.

"Yes, but you were the one who had said that I could freely use the room service. I did just that."

"True! But I had specifically asked you not to sign those bills."

"Okay, okay! I will pay for those bills. Settled?" His tone had picked up a tinge of sarcasm.

"You better!" I said trying to settle the matter, even though I was worried if those invoices would ever be settled. As a precautionary measure, I had made up my mind to collect those specific dues from him.

He was gone for the night even as I contemplated ways to drive the man away.

I only saw him the next evening. Though he seemed to behave like an old wife who wouldn't speak to her husband following a nasty fight, I decided to confront him in the nicest but firmest way possible.

"Adel...." I paused to get his attention and then went ahead. "What do you plan to do now that you haven't managed to get a job in the last six months and...?"

"It will come, don't worry it will," he interjected. "And, I will pay you the rent for the period I stayed here."

"Thank you, I didn't ask for that, but now that you have brought it up, so may I ask how?

"I mean you have nothing left. You have virtually exhausted all your savings, at least that's what you told me," I added.

That's when I offered a suggestion, trying my best to reason in the face of his stubbornness, which could be very overpowering as I had realised while getting to know him in the last few months. "Why don't you instead look for jobs in Jordan? Your entire family stays there; don't you think it would be a better option?"

The answer left me stunned; I could virtually feel the steam rushing out from my ears.

"There aren't any jobs there. Not at least the ones which would let me live the lifestyle that I am used to," he said with underlying unabashedness, which was further augmented by what he did. He pulled out a tissue from the box lying on the centre table, cleaned his nose, and threw it on the table.

"That was it," I thought. My face went red, but I still tried controlling my temper.

That 'nose-picking job' probably hit the nail on the head. Even before I could say a word he had picked up the used tissue and it had found its rightful place in the dustbin.

"Don't worry it will come," he said, attempting to offer an explanation into why it was tough for him to get a job. The agitation on his face told me that there was no point in reasoning with him at that juncture.

I simply said: "This time when you go to Jordan. DON'T COME BACK!" The firmness in the tone didn't elicit any response but, managed to drill my point inside his shaved head.

The next evening I went straight to the hotel's accountant, who by now had become acquainted with me. Being an Indian, he could empathise with my problems. I asked him to check for all the invoices that Adel had signed and provide me with the details.

"You don't have to worry about it, *bhai*," he said, reassuringly. "Till the time you are under your daily limit, you need not worry about those signatures."

I was adamant, so I decided to ask Adel for 1000 Riyals for the time being. To my complete surprise, he didn't offer any excuses and let his wallet do the talking. No wonder, the man had some style and definitely an inflated ego, which came out crystal clear when he said: "If you need more let know." Ahoy!

Adel eventually did go back to Jordan, but the place couldn't hold him for long. We met a month later at the Town Café, which proved to be our last meeting for an hour later he picked up his suitcase from my room and finally, made his way out. Wait a second, it wasn't him who picked up the suit case, but I. He had only picked up his *thob* and suits.

And, one evening when I was with my family in India, enjoying my annual leave. I got a message from him that was copied from an earlier text that I had sent him which read, *"I can't imagine how good for nothing and worthless you have been. I just needed a bit of interpretation help from you and you couldn't make yourself available in time. This isn't the first time I have noticed this attitude in you."*

I had sent the verbal volley to him when I was out looking for a house and Rami, the office *Mandoop* (PRO), was showering me with directions in Arabic (*nah* Egyptian!).

The message was followed by: "What is your account number?"

--x--

MAFI MUSHKILA

I felt like banging my head on the wall that day but instead ended up pulling my hair. Thankfully, they were strong enough to resist the onslaught.

Those repeated 'missed calls' would have driven any person to insanity.

I had immersed myself in an elite lifestyle that comes with staying at a hotel for long. But, one fateful day, a series of missed calls broke the rhythm. Finally, I decided to call back, only to encounter a verbal salvo in a language, which was still alien to me.

The case was even worse than what I had been made to endure by way of my interactions with Mustafa. At least in Mustafa's case, I had the convenience of walking up to his workstation and using Google Translate to get my point across. But the 'luxury' was completely denied on the phone.

All I could say was, "*mafi malum Arabi* (don't know Arabic)". But, the man persisted with his monologue, until I decided to tap the red button on my phone. The sudden silence was delightful. Thinking it to be a 'wrong number' or a case of mistaken identity, I decided to push the incident away from my consciousness and went back to routine.

To my bad luck, the silence was short-lived. That afternoon, even as I was checking my phone on my way back from the office prayer room, the look on my face said it all; there were two missed calls from the same number.

I approached Altaf, the office boy or 'office man' taking into account his age. I dialled the number making sure that he was in close quarters, for I didn't want to get lost in a verbal mishmash again.

That was when I came to know that person who kept giving me missed call was, in fact, Rami, the office *Mandoop*.

An odds jobs man, Rami, would act as a liaison between the Qatar Olympic Committee, government agencies, ministries and bodies especially dealing with Housing and allied projects. In my case, as in the case with most other QOC employees, he had been tasked with the job of looking out for a decent and furnished accommodation.

Altaf informed me that, he had managed to locate a decent accommodation for me in Al Sadd. It also became clear that I had already missed out on an earlier chance to obtain a flat as I could not decipher what Rami was saying.

"Why didn't you take his call earlier?" asked Altaf.

"But, he never called me. They were just missed calls."

"So, you should have called him back," he added.

"I did. But, I couldn't understand what he was saying."

Altaf even told me that the *Mandoop* was upset because I wasn't taking his phone calls.

"What was the point in taking the phone calls," I thought. "I would have hardly understood a word."

So, I had to go and check out the flat that Rami had shortlisted. And, the job had to be done ASAP.

The girl next door (read next office), Rida, eased my anxiety a bit by providing the directions, which I pretended to understand. But, the fact was that I found them rather vague as technically, I was still new to the city. I did manage to take her number for future reference and set out on my journey.

I wasn't exactly happy as heading back at that hour meant spending a whole lot of money on those expensive taxis or waiting for buses, which were few and far between.

Left with no choice, I hired a taxi to get to Al Sadd, but little did I know that taxi drivers in Doha could hardly be trusted with routes and fares. The man wasn't aware of the location or pretended that way, and neither was he using the GPS. End result – I was forced to get down a mile off the desired destination.

So there I was walking even as the blazing sun scorched my skin. I would take small halts in between to figure out the way, often taking directions from fellow pedestrians or shopkeepers. And yes, at times I would even call Rida and Rami, in the latter's case always ensuring that an interpreter, usually a passer-by, was up close.

Eventually, I did manage to reach the destination and went on to check out the flat. As I entered, a dingy smell filled my nostrils. Clearly, it had been locked for days and was only opened to allow me to have a look.

The apartment was vacant and in a dilapidated state with tiles, washbasins, and bathtub broken up. It may have been possible that the last occupant didn't score too high on the courtesy scale or the house was marked for renovation.

Disappointed, I decided to call it a day and headed towards my hotel. On my way back I didn't forget to text Mubarak about the state of affairs. It would have been a minute before that text on WhatsApp Messenger exhibited a blue tick, that my phone started ringing.

Mubarak, who was must have been in the vicinity, decided to pay a visit. He picked me up from my hotel, and we headed towards the said apartment block.

"All this can be fixed," he said, gesturing towards those broken pieces of tiles. More than that there was something else that struck him, which I had failed to notice.

The structure of the building was such that mobile phone network was down to the last bar in that flat. In fact, at most places even that last bar seemed to diminish.

On further investigation and after speaking to the guards there we concluded that the problem was a rather persistent one.

In a jiffy, the flat was struck off our list and next day I was out looking for another one in Al Sadd.

This time, Rami handed me the key to the apartment and on my way back from the office I visited the place.

As I opened the door, the same damp smell greeted me, but the flat was well furnished and to my liking.

I took pictures of the room and sent it back to my wife in India and also forwarded the same to Mubarak.

The next day with the help of another interpreter, I told Rami that I am ready to move in.

"*Mafi mushkila* (no problem)," he said and nodded his head in affirmation, but the 'move in' was still a far cry as I was to realise later.

I was told to go to the housing office with the keys and fill out a couple of forms, which I dutifully did.

A couple of days later I went back to collect copies of the letter which authorised my occupancy. The same I was supposed to deposit at the power and water, along with the required fee towards insurance.

But, it was here that the trouble really began. The meter readings that I had obtained from the flat were most peculiar. They were so unique that even the clerk, a person from Rawalpindi, at the branch office, in Al Sadd failed to understand them.

He performed a check on his computer screen only to shake his head in confusion. At last, he told me to meet the *mudir* (manager). I went upstairs to the manager, who referred the case back to where I had come from – the head office.

Ultimately, the customer care girl at the head office cleared my doubts.

"The last tenant didn't clear the bills. That's why you are seeing such a reading," she said.

Tired and exhausted, I didn't pursue the matter any further and went straight to the office. Once there, I appraised Mustafa about the issues. But, like always he told me to be patient.

"I don't know what to say. Your case is the first of its nature," said a person, who had come to visit us that day.

"Ah! Looks like I am jinxed," I thought and smiled, even though I was too peeved for the same.

In the end, I decided to get Rami involved in the whole business. A few calls to him every day ensured that I was able to move in before the holy month of Ramadan.

--x--

THAT RAMADAN DELICACY

The kitchen cabinet was empty and so was the refrigerator. There was nothing in sight which could have qualified as my personal *Iftar* 'feast'. There may have been a few dates lying in one corner and a piece of *Khubus*, the famous and heavily subsidised Arabic pita bread, which had become my staple diet ever since I had left the hotel, and the 'room service' had become a distant dream. But, I was one of those who relished a hearty *Iftar* and those items were sadly not enough.

I was rediscovering bachelorhood after eight years of enjoying the marital bliss and it wasn't something I had expected. Not at least the way it is romanticised in Hollywood or B-Town flicks. Nor was it any close to those 'distorted' feminists or masculinist ideologies, the latter if there is one, which often put singles on the pedestal even though they would be far removed from reality.

At best my condition would have been close to the protagonist of Renée Zellweger-starrer *Bridget Jones's Diary*, but with an aching and heart-wrenching difference. Bridget, in her early 30s, was on the lookout, while I had reached the age where men start showing signs of hair growth in all sorts of places, but their head, where there is marked decline. In most cases there are hardly any takers for such 'phenomenal male species'.

So, even as I was trying desperately to make ends meet and save a bit for the uncertain future, I was forced to obverse 'temporary celibacy'. Yes, a few make-believe winks may have come my way from the fairer sex, but that's where it ended. Well! For the prude, if at all it matters, I was trying not to cheat on my wife even though there were distractions, which could have left me undone or better put unzipped.

The phone bell got me off to a start; it was from the Information Technology Department of my office. "*Keif al-Hal?* (How are you?)" the soft-spoken voice said.

"Oh! Ghanim, good you called; I really want the issue with my computer resolved."

Though it wasn't protocoled to directly approach a person from the IT Department, I would often use my connections or *wasta* as it is usually called in this part of the world to get my work done. And like always, my Man Friday in the department of the geeks was 'The' trouble-shooter - Ghanim.

So there he was trouble-shooting the problems of my computer.

"Brother, what are you doing post office?" He asked.

"Nothing," I said. The indifference was clearly visible in my voice. I was interested in resolving the problem that was to confront me in the evening – *Iftar*.

I avoided the question trying to focus on which mall I should visit to buy groceries that would last me the entire month of Ramadan.

I tried putting things into perspective by preparing a budget that wouldn't leave my slim wallet drained. Ironic as it would have sounded; the budget was designed to meet my basic need – Live. But then everyone has been doing just that ever since the term 'money' was coined. And if you bring the Biblical proportions into considerations, since the time Adam ate that godforsaken apple.

"*Bhai*!" Ghanim's rather soft-spoken voice, very unlike me, filled the void.

"Why don't you come with me today?"

"But, I have to buy groceries for *Iftar*," I said, trying to find an escape route.

"*Habibi*, don't worry when I am here! I will take you to a place you won't regret."

Habibi, don't worry when I am here! I will
take you to a place you won't regret.

That afternoon Ghanim was carefully heading in his Mitsubishi sedan towards the pre-planned destination with me in the seat meant for the navigator, even though I wasn't providing any navigation.

On the way, he led me into a conversation that centred on food. Though, it seemed a bit odd considering the fact that both of us were on fasts. Nevertheless, I continued listening.

"Have you ever eaten *Harees*," he asked.

"What is that?"

"Brother, it's a special delicacy that is usually prepared during Ramadan. And where I am going to take you today, it is distributed free."

The sentence caused my eye to glint at the prospect of a feast to culminate the laborious first day's fast that had left me exhausted. The thought though enticing enough made me wonder what I would be doing for the rest of the day as the time for *Iftar* was still a couple of hours away.

The car halted near a plush bungalow.

"This is the residence of the Sheikh," said Ghanim, even as he pulled out two wide and deep dishes from a bag that was stacked below the rear seat.

As he led me beyond the open gates, I could see a beeline of men, women and children with dishes and pans in their hands. I could gather what was coming up by the looks of it, but tried not make it obvious by my off-the-cuff remarks.

However, Ghanim gathered it from the expressions on my face. "*Bhai, nakko* worry," he said, punctuating his English with a heavy dose of Hyderabadi. "See there are men coming in suits to collect their day's ration."

"Yes, yes, pretty much."

"But, isn't it weird?"

"Not at all," he explained. "This has been a tradition during Ramadan since as far as I can remember and the Sheikhs are known for their large heart."

A large crowd had gathered near the porch and the Sheikha had stepped out. With a large spoon in her hand, she started the day's proceedings.

As the commotion grew, Ghanim dished out the keys and asked me to sit in the car as he prepared for the task at hand – procurement of good quality of *Harees* in shortest possible time. And there was only one way he could do it. It was by *wasta* (or *jugad* as it is called in New Delhi and regions of northern India), a quick-fix to such issues.

I soon comprehended that the *wasta* involved getting in touch with the Sheikh's driver for the beefy or the greasy part of the *Harees*.

The aroma was so overwhelming that I had to quickly put the dish away, lest it created problems with my fasting.

"What is it made of?"

"It is made up of wheat and meat," he went on. "The wheat is soaked overnight, and then simmered in water along with meat and butter. The ingredients are ground together till they turn into a paste."

"As one would expect, spices and a generous dose of butter ensure that you get that kind of aroma."

Sprinkling the topic with a bit of contemporary history, he said, "It's good that these days the cooks use mechanical grinders for the purpose. There was a time when they would spend the entire day grinding the broth."

"But, they must be professionals."

"Yes, undoubtedly, and they are generously paid too. The task is to prepare the broth in such a fashion that it's light on the stomach but high on energy."

The evening descended and it was time for the great feast. After the customary bit with the dates, I went for the *Harees*. A minute in the microwave and I was ready to gorge on the age-old Arabian delicacy.

Unexpectedly enough, the first morsel got stuck in my mouth. No wonder, the day-long fast had left the interiors of my mouth high and dry. A little water and I were ready for a thorough trial.

Spoon by spoon the taste built on me. The wheat and the meat were so finely mixed that it was difficult to differentiate one from the other, a bit of 'red' in one corner was a giveaway, but on the whole it tasted like porridge. A bit of olive oil would have helped, but it was nowhere in sight, so I continued with the handfuls and mouthfuls. Oddly enough, by the time I was done, I longed for more.

The month witnessed more trips down the track making it well-beaten. And as for the delicacies, *Biryani* or *Majboos*, cakes, dates et cetera followed but, *Harees* beat the rest with its sudden spurt of energy. A natural Red Bull, I'd say!

--x--

THAT FREE RIDE

It was the usual. I was out there, standing at the bus stop when suddenly I noticed a young car driver waving towards me.

Swiftly, I walked towards him and knocked at the car's window. "Five Riyals," I said and made a gesture with my hand, indicating the amount. He rolled down the glass and gave me an answer that left me puzzled.

"Did I ask for money?"

The curt tone that bordered on annoyance would have left me searching for answers, but the "hop in" saved the day.

The fair stranger with sharp features and curls had just offered me a free ride, a rather unusual phenomenon. And that too without an apparent request made me suspicious.

"*Wallah!* Am I dreaming?" made an escape route from my stiff lips, which should have remained sealed.

"No! You are not, definitely not."

His smile was enchanting. Those light eyes looking to play a prank made me sit uptight, alert until he waved again. This time, signalling to my erstwhile fellow bystander, a Filipina well into her 40s. The woman reacted, albeit a millisecond late. The driver tailgating us was low on patience and made no bones about it, showcasing his urgency by honking.

Luckily, for me, it was Doha and not Delhi, for had it been the latter, his prowess at using the horn would have turned into a long and steady innings.

Why many high-end car companies make special models for the Indian market. These cars come with reinforced horns, aimed at satisfying our pleasures derived from high-decibel honking.

A stern look behind, a few more gestures and we were on our way to Souq Waqif.

"I don't know why he was honking so much. They really have no patience. After all, I was just trying to help that lady," said Kamaal, an Egyptian, who used to work in the human resource department of a steel company in Industrial Area.

The overwhelming feeling that came with 'The' free ride was still to sink when a sudden interjection heightened the surprise quotient.

"You know what? That guy must be an Indian. Only Indians honk that much."

"Come on! I was only trying to help that lady, and the man didn't let me do that. One must always help and above all respect women," he stressed.

"By the way, I am an Indian too," I said, trying not to look offended by his observation, which was correct by a large measure.

"Oh is it? Well Actually, I noticed that you are a practising Muslim, and that's why I decided to help you."

"But, how did you know that?" I asked, somewhat surprised. Guess, the day was full of surprises.

"Those marks on your forehead *Habibi* are tell-tale signs."

Stumped at finding myself at the receiving end of an Egyptian's benevolence, I couldn't stop myself from wondering if I had "help me" written in bold on my forehead.

Now, now, I don't intend to sound racist or judgemental here, but the general perception among the Arabs is that no one asks an Egyptian for help.

The reason – they rarely offer a helping hand.

In fact, a Sudanese national, who was on the lookout for a job and had asked me about openings at my office, was left disappointed when he came to know that it required gathering information from an Egyptian.

"Leave it. They don't really help," he had said. "In fact, they will not even help their own countrymen."

Kamaal too admitted. "Yes, I am aware of it," he said.

"Sometimes it can be very frustrating. I too experienced the same issue from my own people when I had taken up this job. It was almost as if I was up against a wall."

The free ride had turned my perception, especially about the Egyptians, on its head.

The Egyptians, second only to Malayalis in Qatar, were men of extreme traits. Either they would be very helpful, going out of their way, or they won't bother at all. Kamaal, I guess, came from the first category.

But, the question that pecked my brain was why did he dislike the Indians? And when I say 'Indians,' I mean Keralites as they are the most dominant community from India based in the Arabian Gulf.

The answer came to me in a flash when Kamaal drove past the Lulu Hypermarket. The massive superstore, which has its footprints, 123 to be precise, in the entire GCC region, is a brainchild of M. A. Yousuf Ali, a Keralite.

The exemplary example of entrepreneurship set by Ali and others like him would no doubt be a sore point for some expatriates. The draconian sponsorship system and strict visa regulations followed by some nations, clearly wasn't a deterrent for Ali.

But then there's no smoke without fire. And it dawned on me that envy wasn't the only reason. Some even say that Keralites aren't noble paymasters. But, then the same might hold good for the rest as a Nepalese labourer had once pointed out.

"They are all the same; it's just the matter of being in that superior position," he had said.

A Kenyan taxi driver, who I met during my first month in Qatar, disliked the idea of Keralites not referring to themselves as Indians, but Keralites.

"You ask them, where are you from and they won't say India. They would say Kerala," he had said. "I don't know why they don't they say India up front."

That Kenyan taxi driver may have formed his opinion based on observations under the prevailing circumstances that can be called "extremely competitive", but had he known of a certain man called Verghese Kurien he would have changed his mind.

Not many are aware that Dr. Kurien, a Keralite, was actually the man behind what Gujarat and, to some extent, what India is today.

Famous for 'Amul Butter', Dr. Kurien had single-handedly turned India from a milk deficient nation into a leading exporter. And how – by a simple idea.

The best ideas are often the simplest and 'duty-free'.

"A key achievement at Amul was the invention of milk powder processed from buffalo-milk abundant in India as opposed to that made from cow-milk in the then major milk producing nations," says Wikipedia, another iconic platform for information, which too is absolutely free.

Today, Amul stockholders come from Anand, the very village where Dr. Kurien started the Operation Flood. He maybe long gone, but his memories remain, etched as they have been on the silver screen by Shyam Benegal in his iconic flick *'Manthan'*.

As for me, I was happy to watch that long queue at the milk booths selling bottled milk run dry. They were replaced by chic packets with informative and interesting reads at shops around the corner.

That free ride had ended, but the class divide amongst the expatriates will probably never end. After all, they constitute more than 85 per cent of the total population of Qatar.

--x--

THAT INCREDIBLE MAN,
WHO HELD MY HAND

It must have been long before he let the mind take over the heart. The *damn* cufflink had become rather stubborn for his liking.

My father, unlike me, relishes the well-groomed look. No wonder, he is known for his penchant for turning up in chic attires at dos, which are frequented by the glitterati of Urdu literature. His nom de plume, Sehba, albeit feminine, is enough for connoisseurs of Urdu poetry to stand up and take notice.

More than two decades have passed, but the incident is still fresh as if it were but yesterday.

The cufflink just kept slipping away, that day.

I sat there and watched the entire episode even as he struggled to get that piece of accessory in place. My lips were sealed, they held off the temptation of uttering the cliché 'May I help?' which in those days would have been akin to blasphemy, considering his temper.

Rooted in his childhood, those bursts of fury would often find a match in an adolescent me – a rebel without a cause.

My father's story, however, was a study in contrast. A freak accident during his boyhood left his arm gravely impaired. By the time his fragile frame made it to the hospital, irreparable damage had been done. The injury had turned his left arm into what now looks like a crooked dry branch of a tree, below the elbow.

The dilemma would have nearly consumed me before the "Son! Won't you help me?" emerged as the saviour. Those words had literally broken the ice, signalling the start of an era of trust between me and my father. It was also the time when my father realised I had come of age and he decided to acknowledge the fact.

In time, his reliance on me grew and I didn't disappoint him either, always standing by his 'left side' to put it literally.

Adolescence passed and I stepped into adulthood. Higher education followed by demands of the job, and finally marriage changed the equation between us.

Soon, my wife and I decided to buy an apartment on the outskirts of New Delhi and one fine day, decided to move in. From then on, a visit to the parents had become a weekend luxury, until that too turned into a distant dream when I took up the job in Doha.

The man who had begun to rely on me would have been heartbroken to hear the news but, like always, didn't make it apparent until I returned home for Eid al-Fitr. It was then that I was made to hear a series of suggestions, all aimed at tying me down in India. Some of them valid, others I could have contested. But as the days passed they were all forgotten, leave alone challenged. And, pressing matters of the financial and legal nature assumed importance. Papers that had been gathering dust at government offices and courts were shown the light of the day. Most were self-attested, some cost me my flab, still others turned my wallet ultra slim. The rest were just pushed under the 'some other time' category.

Unplanned get-togethers with friends and family, an impromptu alumnus meet, a short visit to Nagpur, and my holidays were exhausted much before I did.

So there I was getting ready to pack my bags even as my phone bell kept ringing. In most cases the person on the other end would yield the oft quoted, "Man, you couldn't find time for me" phrase, but a select few did manage to spare time even during the eleventh hour. Quite frankly those few were the ones who mattered, the rest were merely doing lip service.

Hours turned into minutes and I was in Doha on schedule.

It took me a considerable time to get back to the routine warding off those nostalgic pangs. Gradually, the dullness took over and the 'work as usual' made me tide over my emotions. That heart-to-heart talk that I had with my father in India was conveniently pushed down the deep and intricate alleys of my mind. They would have stayed there, but for that jolt by an unlikely catalyst, which left me in a retrospective mood.

A drop of sweat trickled down Chinese Paralympian Zhou Hongzhuan's nose as she raced to the finish in the women's 1500 T54 wheelchair heats at the 2015 IPC Athletics World Championships.

The camera panned across her face with that droplet sitting pretty on that precise spot where a lady would lovingly wear a nose stud, except in her case it was sweat, which glistened like gold amidst the amber lights. As luck would have it, Zhou did end up with the real gold, the one that hung around her neck while she sported a million-dollar smile.

And even as everyone stood in silence when the Chinese national anthem was being played, my mind raced back to that moment in time when that gold-plated cufflink had slipped off his hand and trundled into the ray of sunshine, that made it sparkle.

The "son, won't you help me?" echoed in my mind. It was almost as if I were transported back home and he was right there standing beside me.

That's when it dawned upon me, "Did he really want my help?" After all, my mother was there too. Or was he trying to suggest something? Something, which was so profound, that it could not be put into words.

Was he trying to bridge that gap between him and a teenager, who could have gone astray?

Only he knows the answer, but something that I have come to know after all these years is that it wasn't him, but I, who needed the helping hand. Certainly not him!

As for Zhou, she ended with two more silvers around her neck.

A drop of sweat trickled down Chinese Paralympian
Zhou Hongzhuan's nose as she raced to the finish

My eyes darted across the banner that read: "Beyond Incredible!"

--x--

HERE COMES THE SUN

For me, it definitely was cheating of the highest order, or lowest, if I were to put exhibitionism on a yardstick.

Wonder, why her profession wasn't 'classified' under the laws governing consumer affairs? After all, every act of hers was intended for, if I am allowed to say, "Satisfaction", albeit of a different orientation, but satisfaction all the same.

So there I was deprived of a few good things in life and struck down to the bed, recuperating from flu and allied illnesses. And when you are prescribed drugs with 'Made in Egypt' or 'Made in Switzerland' declarations, you do know that something isn't how it should have been. It also means that either your mind or your body is thwarting the change or is taking too long to adjust to the surroundings.

Speak to a 'natural born expat'. Yes, there are a few born in the commotion that arises from the confluence of societies. A man of such a trait would tell you that the right time to venture into this transition is during the 20s. And, I had not only crossed that figure by a mile but, added decades to it, before the metamorphosis could actually happen.

My case would be akin to a certain Mr. Anderson of *'The Matrix'* fame, who had become Neo rather too late in life. Before that, of course, he was content, if not happy in his present state of affairs.

But, unlike him, I hadn't been delivered that shock of 'the Lady in Red' that had virtually given him a jump start. So there I was trying to make do with those 'Made in Egypt' medicines to get rid of the most mundane of illness but, instead, what I actually needed was a jump start *aka* 'satisfaction'.

Besides, the intermittent showers and the sudden change in weather had ensured that my bed rest was optimised to the maximum.

"It rains in winters!" I had said with marked exclamation while giving instructions to a friend, who was packing for his short Doha sojourn. But, to be honest, the runny nose on Skype would have sufficed.

Not an unusual phenomenon for people living in the Arabian Gulf, with many hoping for rains during the season but, for someone used to tropical climes like New Delhi, it definitely was disconcerting.

So as things stood or rather slouched that day, I was cold and alone in my large apartment. It had rained cats and dogs the last night and I hoped for the sunshine. I drew the curtains only to have my senses clouded by the gloom. The dark clouds were looming large and the weather forecast didn't shed any light either, in the literal sense.

I went through the paces even as those little 'ting, tings' on my phone, told me that there'd be some action trending on the cyberspace if not the real world.

I prepared some breakfast. With dishes in my hands and the phone in my pocket I sat in front of the telly, looking forward to some entertainment. Unfortunately, that too turned out to be a downer. The bad weather had ensured that the TV was out of the picture and reduced to what many would call the 'idiot box'.

So it had to be just the phone and me now. After doing away with those undesirable group texts on WhatsApp Messenger, I tried calling my wife. Unfortunately, there was no response from the other side.

Without much thought, my finger tapped the Facebook icon and there I was drawn into a suggested page that just showed up out of nowhere. The description said 'Actor/Director' with 17 million likes. Without a doubt, the woman was a celebrity.

In fact, she was so big a celebrity that she had outdone many a star from the tinsel town merely by displaying her assets, that too meagrely. Often her skin would be depicted as flawless, marble-like, which men from the advertising world would use to sell products. As for the 'Actor/Director' part, there definitely was room for improvement.

"But then, when you have skin like hers why would you act?" I wondered. All she needed to do was stand in the shower and let those tiny droplets of water slide over her gorgeous body with the camera angles playing tricks in the hands of an expert lens man – hiding most of those contours and revealing just a tiny bit to let the mind do the fantasising.

I am told that a few gentlemen often addressed as 'gurus' are such experts that they could not only turn the undesirable into desirable but, could raise the bar with regards to the oomph factor without much ado.

In fact, some could even use innocent and harmless props like water droplets to bamboozle their audience into submission. Perhaps, an increase in the resolution of those droplets to make them appear like golf balls filled with juicy liquid caressing model's well-oiled skin was an open secret. The rest, as they say, is Photoshop.

*"Publicity though negative is
publicity all the same!"*

Earlier, a promotional video from her recent flick came up on my WhatsApp Messenger. The scantily clad curvaceous actress was shown gyrating to a very suggestive tagline, which left me in splits.

The video became an instant hit on social networking sites. Ironically, for her, it became so successful that it turned out to be overkill, and as a result, the movie went down with a whimper at the Box Office.

"How can people make such movies," I wondered.

Still she continued to hog the limelight as a socialite. If that wasn't enough a particular television journalist, known to me since college, had utilised the hot bod to peddle his programme to an audience, which would on any given day sleep through the whole charade.

The man, I am told, was happy with the spike in the TRPs even as his poster doubled up as a dartboard for certain sections of the society.

"Publicity though negative is publicity all the same!" I thought and a smile slipped across my rather sullen face, battered under the influence of bad weather, lack of sleep, 'zero television' and 'sporadic' bowel movements.

Out of curiosity, I turned towards to her Facebook page. But, my eagerness quickly dwindled and an unpardonable hatred assumed its presence when images after images came up with virtually no skin show, whatsoever.

Okay! There may have been that 'average' presentation of the skin in a few pictures, but that definitely didn't go with her much-publicised 'oomph-lified' image. In fact, even the condom advertisements displayed there were rather sober.

Imagine what impact would such an advertisement elicit that has a pornographic star-turned-Bollywood hot bod holding a coffee mug with a tagline which starts with, 'The perfect date' and then goes on to add 'coffee' and ends with a 'chocolate'. Wonder, if it was Valentine's Day when those series of advertisements were conceptualised, for they seemed more mushy than sensual. Accepted, that there was a bit of exposure in that one, but had it not been for that brand name, I would have mistaken it for a coffee or a chocolate advertisement. After all, there have been advertisements promoting shoes with more skin show to boast off.

"How can a character like her be covered from head to toe," I thought, horror-struck at the complete makeover she had been doing to her image ever since she made her foray into feature films.

However, the B-Town producers it seems are still stuck with her former image much like that television journalist, who had run out of synonyms for the word 'past' while firing questions at her.

But, when someone's past is as glorious as hers, who would look at her present, which like the iconic scooter brand of yesteryears, would need a bit of bending to get a kick-start.

I decided to shun her and move on to a young brigade of 'lifeguards' during those unglorified days of 'temporary celibacy'.

Besides, I didn't have a choice. As a famous septuagenarian actor, whose Facebook likes resemble a telephone number had provided an apt explanation in a critically acclaimed Bollywood flick.

En route to meet the father of his love interest – the female lead, almost half his age, asks the most vital question: "How would you approach my father?"

It's the conversation that ensued summed up my situation even though I was younger than the female protagonist when the film was shot.

"I'd be very simple and say it all," he responds.

"No, no, but tell me what would you say?" she prods.

The answer was creative beyond comparison.

"Only this that our body's sexual centre is located in the hypothalamus and that is situated in the brain. The hypothalamus controls our heart, blood pressure and emotions."

He goes further. "Among the men the hypothalamus is slightly bigger and if it is kept away from sex for rather too long, it fails to control itself and in a fit of rage, the blood pressure and heart rate increases and the man dies. That's why I intend to marry your daughter Neena as my hypothalamus has gone berserk."

My hypothalamus may not be as large as his, but I could still do with those lifeguards.

The weather had cleared and the sun was out.

The actress, meanwhile, was spotted amongst the cricketers. The male contraceptive brand she endorses is a sponsor for a highly-acclaimed T20 cricket team.

--x--

LOVE ACROSS THE CYBERSPACE

It was sufficiently clear that I had jumped the gun. And it wasn't the first time I had done it. My blunt and brash self, with little self-control, had shattered her self-respect beyond repair.

Don't know what came over me that day, for I decided to mouth words which were more than inappropriate, especially given her state of mind. They wouldn't have gone down well with even the most thick-skinned women if, there are any for that matter. The result was an array of verbs from her end which, were obviously hard for me to digest.

My sentence was virtually reduced to so..., ah no..., that's not..., I am extremely....But, the deed was done and there was no point in crying over spilt milk.

The phone went dead and the silence was killing. Repeated checks on WhatsApp Messenger too turned futile. The misery was so great that phantom rings would wake me up in the middle of the night and all I could do was stare into the 'blue' of my phone.

The breakup with Aditi had broken me.

This despite the fact that I was 'supposedly' happily married to my wife based 1600 miles away in Delhi. Wonder, if they have a name for such marriages with the flyer miles thrown in!

The depression was gaining in mass and momentum like that ball of ice that hurtles down the hill, flattening anything and everything that comes in the way. But then I wasn't an adolescent, who would have been squashed by such trivialities.

The retrospective streak that had gradually begun to draw me out of the depressing tailspin suddenly delivered a sucker punch, blasting off the negativity. I wondered, which woman would overtly praise her own derriere, and that too with unparalleled enthusiasm like Aditi had done. The thought made me justify my action and soon I was back to my usual self with renewed vigour.

But wait, the thought, albeit laced with sexism, had occurred to me after I had been dumped. "Ah man, was she suggesting something or I was just being stupid?"

The shock made me reconstruct the turn of events.

"I don't know what's wrong with men; they just keep looking at my butt. Guess it's too large." Her voice, though groggy, was seductive but sleepy that I was, failed to gather the cues.

"Let them see. You should be happy that it is helping those poor deprived souls," I said. "It's akin to social work." I had said, trying to sound intellectual even though it was nothing short of foolishness. There I was talking about the birds and bees with someone, who definitely had loads of experience, or at least that's the way she projected herself. With one failed marriage and one live-in, she definitely had been in the thick of things at a not-so-old age of 29.

But, what emerged from her approach was the definite slant she had towards the intellectual types and that's where I scored. Or at least, I presented myself that way, with the paraphernalia that is attached to being a scribe.

We connected on the cyberspace and even before our 'thing', if it could be classified that way, could enter the realistic world it had evaporated.

I had spotted her on Inter Nations, a community for expats. An invitation and a few clichéd salutations later our story had begun, or at least I assumed it did.

After all, we did provide the broadband and data service providers in Doha a platform to make money. We would talk over the WhatsApp Messenger for hours with a special focus on weekends when there would be a distinct spike in data usage.

It was during such a talkathon that she provided me an insight into her relationships. One such affair had started off in Mumbai when she had stepped into puberty and culminated in 'child marriage'. An unfortunate miscarriage followed by intermittent verbal spats, which got regular over a period of time. Her husband, who did odd jobs, failed to pay off the mounting bills and resorted to physical abuse. Surprisingly, the story seemed like a plot from a run-of-the-mill 80s Bollywood movie.

I think the 'damsel in distress' tactic was rather intoxicating for my gullible self. The age-old formula may have been well-beaten, but it found a taker, as I readily accepted whatever Aditi blurted out. "My tale is such that you could do an entire book on it," she had said.

Accepted that she was very young at the time of marriage and could do little in the face of exploitation, but why would she commit another mistake far more damning than the previous one and that too as an adult was beyond my imagination. Whether it was the craving for a house or a family or the much-needed financial stability, whatever it was, Aditi had obviously picked the wrong men – the smooth talkers.

No wonder her WhatsApp Messenger status: "If a man comes up to you and promises the world, punch that lying bastard on the face and run," provided an insight into her personal life.

I still clearly remember the first time that I spoke to her on the phone was following her break-up. "Okay! I have shed my tears and the feeling is out of the window," she had said. Surprisingly though, her tone didn't exhibit any signs of the emotional wear and tear that her heart and mind would have endured only moments ago. Call her strong-willed, but there could be a generic explanation for that. And chances are it stemmed from the fact that she had been an NRI (Non Resident Indian) for too long to effectively numb down the pressures of such genus. Expatriates, believe it or not, face adversity that regular blokes fail to even comprehend.

In fact, the rich and famous have often been quoted and unquoted on perils of life as an expat.

"We NRIs are made to sweat in places that friends back home have no clue about." The generic statement by Ghanim, the portly colleague from IT department, fittingly described Aditi's state of mind.

She continued. "You see, I am one of those who fall for the intellectual types."

Before she could have completed the sentence, I blurted out: "In that case you ought to try my father. He definitely fits the bill."

Aditi broke into a laughter making me realise that despite my age, I could still hold out against the young guns in certain finer nuances of the game of flirting.

So that's how we connected on the cyberspace with WhatsApp Messenger becoming the delivery boy for chunks of data, mostly voice-based.

As the days went by I had begun to sympathise with her.

In fact, that night, the long-drawn conversation had left me so emotionally drained that I was forced to seek a friend's help to tide over the gloom. A tough task when you are a loner amidst the hordes of men. Literally too, considering the skewed sex ratio of expats in the country.

Call it her Bong roots or the upbringing, her attraction towards the intellectual types was understood.

"Physically, the guy was nothing. But, it was his Ph.D. that got me," said Aditi, about her recent unsuccessful relationship with the 45-year old African-American.

"I enjoyed his company. We would sit for hours and discuss varied topics."

"I was completely swept off my feet," she added.

Ironic it sounds, but the fact was that the smooth talker had outwitted the Human Resource bigwig in her own backyard and went a step further. The old fellow not only bagged a cushy job but, also bagged her. And the saga didn't just end there, for after the man had left her, his adolescent son too started eyeing her. That's when the woman decided to call it off.

But then the affair had another side to it. For Aditi might have been dreaming of settling in the 'land of the free is the home of the brave', which never came by, not with the smooth talker in her arms. What did come up, was the news that the fellow had another wife based in Bahrain.

So there I was forced to work alongside
a strikingly beautiful woman

And, I was left wondering if I had lost that touch, or was it my conscience that had been infected by a severe dose of dopamine originating from my wedlock of over a decade.

But, yes there definitely was a change in my behaviour as I started putting to test the age old method of interacting with the PYTs. It was the eye contact. Surprisingly, though, it was the very feature that would make my heart pound. In fact, I had once even admitted it to my wife when she had complained why I avoid eye contact even while addressing her.

"I feel shy," I had said, but there may have been other reasons as well. Maybe her eyes were pretty or probably they were so incisive that would bore a hole into my soul. I fail to pinpoint what it was, but it certainly did make me uncomfortable even after spending all those years with her.

Still, I went ahead and gave it a shot at the first available opportunity that came during the AIPS Congress. An event that witnessed the convergence of sports writers from across the globe in Doha.

It also brought in its fold striking women from across the four corners of the world. Guess the statement from a friend from New Delhi more than described the scenario.

"Brother, how do you manage to concentrate on your job amidst such a lavish spread (of beauty)?"

"Ever since I got off the flight, the phenomenon has just multiplied," he had said, with awe. "What is with this place that attracts beauties like a flower does to bees," he presented the unique, but appropriate perspective.

So there I was forced to work alongside a strikingly beautiful woman from the Maghreb, who could have put Aishwarya Rai to shame.

And believe it or not, sparks flew. But, soon enough they subsided when it became known that I was a married man well over the hill, even though I didn't seem so at first glance.

"What do you mean... Taken," was all she had voiced and my heart just sunk into a bottomless pit.

I was definitely shaken and stirred too and it took me the guts of a woolly mammoth to tide over the feelings.

Luckily, the workload during the event helped, and I finally emerged victorious in the battle of the heart and mind. But, there definitely was a catalyst involved that helped me sail beyond the depressing scenario. And once again the WhatsApp Messenger played a pivotal role, but on this occasion, it brought with it glad tidings.

All of a sudden, I connected with a beautiful woman miles away in New Delhi.

Surprisingly enough, she too was 29 but, married with a toddler son.

It was a poem that she had posted in a group that made me take notice. Its verses had virtually laid my heart bare and what followed left my neurotransmitters charged with zillions of ions. It felt as if I was looking at myself in the mirror. It was something, which could be described as being on the cusp of paranormal. A doppelgänger of thoughts, she could just read my mind. And, by the time I could figure out what to say, a suggestion would have popped up on my chat window.

"Man! How could she have known what I was feeling?" I was left wondering at the eerie turn of events. Almost as if she was hacking into my mind.

Days followed and that singular phenomenon associated with her continued to haunt me, until one day I succumbed to my disposition and blurted, "Who the hell are you?"

Those words were hardly enough to hide the dilemma that had besieged me.

"What!" She shot back as if being pulled out from a deep trancelike state.

"What do you mean?"

"Are you a hacker? That's what I mean."

"Guess, I am the voice that you have been searching for all your life." Her calm voice, as if coming from a distance, added to the melodrama of the night.

"But there's something weird about this whole scenario," I retorted.

"And what is that?"

"This doesn't feel real. I mean, how can two people hit it off on WhatsApp Messenger?"

"Well dear, sorry to disappoint you. We just did." She reasoned like an advocate out there to defend a case.

"Call me your Soulmate," her answer had left me undone.

From there on a journey started that was surreal, to say the least. Moments simply rolled over and days flew past my banal existence, which had suddenly turned exciting.

There wasn't a particular time or phase where I could put a 'stop' or 'period', for the conversations were fluid and unending. The effect was so dramatic that once I had to pinch myself to make sure if I were but, awake. It was as if the soul had stepped out from my body and leading me towards my salvation.

Amidst all this, I noticed that there was a welcome change in my character. A predominant calmness was gradually setting in. The negativity, which my detractors always complained about, had quietened down. The math was my negatively charged ions had infused to generate a positive influx.

Above all, I had found the ever-elusive peace. Of course, my story too had the omnipresent magical wand. Call it ironic, but it was designed by an expatriate who, like me, was searching for a home away from home.

Jan Koum, eventually, did find a home for himself but, what I found was priceless – a Soulmate.

The cyberspace, they say, is a devil's hideout and 'www' stands for '666' in Hebrew, which is known to be the mark of the beast or the demon. But then if the demon is there, so should there be angels.

Had I found one?

--x--

IT AIN'T OVER TILL THE
FAT LADY SINGS

"18.24. That's the last I can give you, Sir," the clerk at the nearby currency exchange outlet had said.

"A person transferred 29 thousand today, I gave him the same figure," he said, even as the teller machine at one end of his desk whizzed past my paltry sum. I had decided not to bargain too much and settle for the figure he had quoted. It wasn't too bad either as in the morning XE.com, the Canadian online currency converter, had displayed 1 QAR = 18:34 INR.

The off day for the bourses in the West had ensured that I didn't have to worry about the frequent changes in the conversion rates. And, I had an uncanny feeling that Monday would be ominous. Besides, the final week of the month isn't an appropriate time to send money home, especially when the markets are on a selling spree, pulled down by the spike in the number of 'family maintenance' transfers.

As expected, the next day the Riyal fell and the downward momentum continued for the entire week. Luckily, I had steered clear of the effects of the temporary slump. Surprisingly, though, my brain seemed to work rather well in this department, for numerous times my absent-mindedness has cost me dear.

In fact on one occasion, while climbing up the stairs to my residence, I inserted the key into a door that looked like mine. The difference, however, lay in the number and floor. Only when the door did not open that I realised my folly. The said door was exactly below my flat but, on floor number six. At another occasion, I got off the lift and walked off, only to be pointed out that it was five and not seven, where I resided. Had I not looked around for overtly obvious cues, which too were minimal, I would have got into an argument with the man, who had rectified my error.

Possibly, being an expat and living alone was taking a toll on my cognitive abilities. It seemed as if the brain cells required to carry out the simplest of tasks had gone on an indefinite strike. Surprisingly, though, the tough tasks appeared the easiest.

Even Willy, the registration agent at a popular driving school, had pointed out this strange anomaly during one of my visits to his office. According to his bizarre logic, it was this very reason that I had not been able to procure a driving license till date. This despite the fact that, I had been trying for more than a year now. "I think it's because you are too bright," he had said, making it sound rather weird. "You consider such odd jobs as worthless and that's why don't focus on them." A surprise observation considering that I was meeting him after long. The last time I interacted with him was on WhatsApp Messenger and, that too was a good three months ago.

A few of my brain cells may have developed hostility towards my body, but the rest were still loyal and holding the fort against the rebels. So, I didn't brood over Willy's observation until something showed up on my Gmail that made me stand up and take notice. Call it coincidental or pin it down to 'what's trending', but that Quora question: "Is drowning or burning to death less painful?" was definitely not an ordinary query.

So, was the word 'death' actually trending that day or had it been spurred on by the depressing news from India? A famous television actress had hanged herself to death and it was enough to steal the limelight off a certain students' union leader in New Delhi, who had been fighting for causes, which were unclear to me.

And, there I was sparing a thought towards my state of affairs with special reference to my dysfunctional grey area that was witnessing a loss in memory and cognitive abilities, supposedly a sign of depression. Like always the social networking sites provided a platform for processing those thoughts through countless articles on the incident and the reasons behind her said move, all of which suddenly started trending.

I would hardly take note of Quora or Pinterest posts for that matter except when there's some topic that demands attention like this one, even though I was too naïve to understand why that question showed up until I checked my Feeds: "Photography, Sports, History, Psychology, Music."

Being a Psychology major, it was but an obvious choice, but then who would have expected that something as ghastly as this would show up under the 'Psychology' classification. The answers provided, though scientific, were definitely bloodcurdling. Horrific comparisons, arguments, and counterarguments between the two forms of fatalities knew no bounds.

"Most people don't die from being burned, but rather the inhalation of deadly gases that are caused by fire," A person observed.

A certain self-proclaimed bibliophile had even quoted Sebastian Junger's book 'The Perfect Storm', to describe that drowning feeling. And like the book and the movie by the same name, her description was rather dramatic, even though there's little drama in dying.

I penned down my answer, which was based on experience and not hearsay. As expected the answer become an instant hit with views and 'up votes' shooting up by the hour. Oddly enough, the person who had quoted Junger decided to delete hers. And though it contained a lot of scientific jargons, her answer did ring a bell at least towards the end when she said, "Calmness comes to you eventually, a biological peace as your brain begins to shut down."

My mind raced back to the start of the century when my drive for sports journalism was still singular and not impinged by the 'tricks of trade'. Also, as a young reporter for New Delhi-based tabloid the *Delhi Mid-Day*, I would love to take out time for extracurricular activities.

That's when I was struck by the swimming bug. Technically speaking, I was too old to learn the sport, or for that matter anything that involved disciplining my motor skills. Nevertheless, I took the plunge. And then I was urged on by my fellow swimmers. "If you are not scared, you learn it pretty quickly," they would tell me, making me swell with pride on my foolhardiness.

But, my recklessness paid off, and I picked up the sport in two weeks, give or take a few days. Of course, there were a few ifs and buts; like I would have to be reminded that I wasn't all arms and that the legs weren't limbs but rudders in the pool. Rest as they say is history.

Ironically enough, one of the guys who gave me that *gyan* (lesson), had been trying for two years and still hadn't picked it. I suppose it was the 'fear factor', or the lack of it, that had been a game changer for me.

From being a rookie, I wanted to make a quick transition to being a pro and started pushing the limits and went forth to where the pool was the deepest.

A few more days and 'been there, done that' sensation was getting to my nerves. What the heck, I had even participated in "who gets to the other end first" thing, when one eventful day I was shaken out of my foolishness.

But, that day was different.

The heavy workload at the office had ensured that I was drained even before I started off. In fact, I was so tired that I could have replaced veteran actor Javed Jaffery in the iconic Hamdard's Cinkara commercial, which was a hit on Indian telly in the 1980s:

"Poor chap so overworked
At this rate, he will collapse
Oh dear, oh dear he's had it!
What he needs is a tonic
Oh! He needs something much stronger
Hamdard's Cinkara"

Don't know what came over me. Not only did I venture into the pool, I headed towards the deep. The first two laps were nice and slow, and I didn't feel the strain until it came to me like a jolt. My arms and legs won't propel me any further. The tiles at the other end seemed close, so I tried harder, but like a mirage they just wouldn't come any near.

I wanted to call out for help, but my mind said, "It's only a few inches away. Go for it." Unfortunately, I was done but, the few inches had remained undone. The voice got choked, my senses – mouth, eyes, ears – all flooded with water. A few more anxious moments and panic had set in.

Yes, as Junger had noted, I too tried holding the breath, but those arms and legs just won't push me any further. Ultimately, I gave in.

The weird part was there was some strange form of stillness that had set in. I can't really describe what that was, but it was calm nevertheless. Suddenly, I found myself coughing on the pool sidewalk. The lifeguard had spotted me and pulled me, grabbing my trunks by his hand.

No one said a word. Chances are many didn't even take notice. I picked up my bag and left...

I was shaken, but I didn't forget to visit the pool the next day.

My near death experience may have come by way of an accident, but the depressed actress, who committed suicide, may have encountered the same feelings before her brain decided to give up on her. It must have said a countless 'NOs' and 'save me'. Unfortunately, there wasn't anyone to stop her.

"Gosh! Am I suffering from depression?"

"Is the silent killer creeping on to me, slowly?"

Those thoughts made me recollect my recent visit to a clinic. The Egyptian doctor, pointing his finger towards his temple, had asked me "Are you suffering from stress?"

Though I had replied in the negative, but her suicide made me re-consider.

Luckily, a reassurance with a novel touch by a close friend made me think otherwise.

"Do you think I am suffering from depression?" I had asked.

"No, relax Mr. Bean!" She said helping me recall the Dubsmash App video I had sent to my daughter, Nashrah, for her birthday. My mimicry of the very popular Ronan Atkinson's onscreen character not only cleared my doubts but put me in good spirits.

Later, it emerged that it was not the brain, but the belly that needed immediate attention. Suffering, as I was from acute gastroenteritis or stomach flu. The ailment, though common, was definitely worrisome.

Well technically, I should have been inclined to feel better, if not great, about the fact that my problem was commonplace. On the contrary, I felt otherwise as Gaviscon, the over-the-counter drug for the problem, was selling like hotcakes. Each time I would visit the pharmacy shop, I would be given a clichéd response: "It's sold off."

This was when I hadn't spotted the very effective Indian antacid, Eno, at the local grocery store.

As for Gaviscon, such was its popularity that the pharmacy company producing it had started including a host of flavours to it.

Even otherwise gastroenteritis has assumed significance these days with most doctors referring to it as a lifestyle related problem. Besides, the topic isn't just confined to chemists, druggist, doctors and patients, for it has moved on to the celluloid screen. The flick 'Piku', where Bollywood biggie Amitabh Bachchan is seen brooding over the problem both theoretically and practically, does more than just touch the heart; it strikes a chord with the gut and colon as well.

An Indian doctor at the same clinic did prescribe drugs to deal with my stomach bug that had overgrown into a depression of sorts. But, there hardly was a doctor, who could prescribe a drug to arrest the depression that had been brought on by the plummeting crude oil prices. And for the expats living in the largely oil-fuelled economies, there wasn't a breather. Not that I knew of, even as their drawn faces bore tell-tale marks of the economic upheaval.

On the other side of the spectrum were the investors, who waited in the wings. They knew their time had come.

Pink slips are flying thick and fast even as I'm busy contemplating my future. To rise or perish, only time will tell. After all, it ain't over till the fat lady sings!

ENDS

Printed in the United States
By Bookmasters